THE UNEXPECTED

A novel by
FABIAN LONG

The Unexpected

First published by PACENI 360 Leadership Services

ISBN 978-0-9846507-6-7

Printed in the United States of America.

This book is printed on acid-free paper.

PACENI 360

PACENI 360 Leadership Services
695 Pepperbush Drive
Myrtle Beach, SC 29579
Paceni360@aol.com
www.paceni360.org

ACKNOWLEDGEMENTS

All I would like to thank is God, because if it weren't for him, it would be no me or you.

THE UNEXPECTED

CHAPTER 1

Barbara came home from work early one Friday afternoon after a long week at the job to realize the lights had been turned off.

Lord knows I gave Carl the money to pay this darn bill, she thought to herself.

Reaching for her cell phone, she commenced to call Carl, but like always, there was no answer. So, Barbara left a message telling him the lights were out and that the kids would be home from school soon. Then she sat and patiently waited for him to return her call. Finally, he called back.

"You didn't listen to the message?" she said upon answering the phone.

In a frustrated tone, he yelled, "Hell no! I'm busy!"

"Carl, what did you do?" she asked peacefully. "Did you forget to pay the light bill?"

There was only silence on the other end as Carl hesitated with an answer.

"I know I gave you the money," she continued.

He replied, "Didn't you get paid today?"

"Yes," Barbara responded.

"Well, hell, pay the damn bill! Don't keep calling me with the bullshit!" And with that, Carl hung up in her ear.

Feeling like she was left with no other choice since she didn't want her children to be in the dark, Barbara called a cab so she could go to the bank and pay the light bill before the kids arrived home.

Lord knows I try to do all I can to keep this family together, while Carl steadily pulls us apart, she thought during the cab ride to the bank.

When Barbara got to the bank, she found a long line, with only two tellers open. Time was steadily ticking. She started to worry because there was an hour until the light company closed. No way could she make it there and back before the kids got home.

Barbara flipped open her phone to call Old Man Johnson, the neighbor who lived beneath them, to ask if he could watch the kids until she got there. It was just her luck that he didn't answer. She continued to call as she waited in line to pay her bill. After trying several time to reach him, Old Man Johnson finally picked up.

"Hello. This is Barbara from upstairs. I was wondering if you could watch the kids until I get home."

Old Man Johnson replied, "I would be more than happy to, Mrs. Barbara."

"Thank you! Thank you so much. I will soon return the favor."

"Oh, that will not be necessary. I would love to watch the kids. You have wonderful kids, and they are well mannered. So, take your time."

Barbara thanked him again before hanging up.

Meanwhile, Carl was on his way home from drinking and losing all the bill money at Joe's Poker Shack. When he arrived home to find no one there, he went into a rage, ranting about nothing having been cooked and the kids not being home. He cracked open a cold beer and waited impatiently for his wife to come home.

After a hectic day of trying to get the light bill paid at the last minute, Barbara finally arrived home. She knocked on Old Man Johnson's door to find the kids were having the best time of their lives.

"Did my kids give you a hard time?" she asked Old Man Johnson.

"Of course not. I love your kids. I use to have a family of my own, until the day they left and never came back."

"You mind if I ask what happened?"

"Not at all," Old Man Johnson said. "I have been trying to be at peace with myself now for over twenty years. My wife and three kids were on their way to see me while I was working on a bridge in New York City. We were so backed up with work that we were not able to come home for months at times. They wanted to see me, and I was stressed to see them, too."

Old Man Johnson paused to look at Barbara with a cold look in his eyes as he continued.

"Barbara, I've been blaming myself for many years because I knew my wife was unable to drive far. She had never left the state of South Carolina. But, being selfish, I made her drive anyway. Well, while on the way up here, she turned down a one-way street and had a head-on collision with an eighteen-wheeler. My whole family was killed instantly. When I received the call from the coroner, I went into a state of depression immediately. I've been contemplating suicide each and every day for years. I even lost my job because I couldn't focus. I started blaming God and asking why he would take my family away from me when I did everything I was supposed to do as a father, a husband, and a man."

Noticing that Old Man Johnson was about to break down, Barbara told him, "Everything will be alright. You have a new family now, but I know we can never replace your own. You can see the kids anytime you want, though."

Old Man Johnson wiped the tears from his eyes and said to her, "I apologize for that. It's just sometimes it still hurts."

"I've cried myself, but I always keep the faith believing that God has a plan for us, and one day, he's going to see us through. Well, got to go now and get these kids something to eat. I know they're starving."

Old Man Johnson nodded and said, "Thanks for letting me watch the kids and for making me part of the family." He smiled softly as they walked out the door.

As Barbara gathered the children to leave, Carl Jr. got up slowly. He wanted to tell Old Man Johnson just how much it meant to him, his brother, and his sister to have someone like Old Man Johnson in their lives.

As they walked upstairs, Carl Jr. seized the moment. "Mr. Johnson, can I tell you something?"

"Go ahead, my friend," he responded.

"My sister, brother, and I are glad to have you as a part of our lives, because for so long, our dad has never been there for us, and he's always giving our mother a hard time."

Old Man Johnson looked at Carl Jr., and with a genuine tone, he said, "Don't worry. I promise I won't let anything happen to any of y'all." He then hugged Carl Jr. and added, "I've lost one family, and I won't lose another. Call me anytime you want."

By the time Carl Jr. finished talking with Old Man Johnson, Barbara had walked into the house and was greeted by Carl in a rage.

"Where the hell have you been?" Carl yelled. "And why wasn't the food cooked?"

"Did you forget that someone didn't pay the light bill? I had to take the check I had set aside for Shakira's birthday party to pay it."

Carl yelled back, "Don't come to me about no fuckin' birthday party bullshit when you know these bills come first."

"I know my responsibility!" Barbara replied in an angry tone. "Obviously you don't know yours. I gave you the money a week ago to pay it, and you didn't. So, don't come telling me about what comes first."

Before she could get the next word out, Carl hauled off and slapped her as hard as he could. "Don't you ever...ever in your life come off on me like that! I'm the damn man of this house, and you're going to respect that."

Carl Jr. stood there in shock, along with his sister and brother. This was the first time they had seen their father put his hands on their mother. Being the oldest and wanting to protect his siblings, Carl Jr. grabbed Michael and Shakira and took them in the other room so they wouldn't have to witness their my mother get hit again. Carl Jr. locked the door behind him after getting Michael and Shakira inside, and then they sat in the corner of the dark closet while crying a river.

Carl continued yelling and hitting Barbara. Feeling helpless and not knowing what he could do to protect his mother, Carl Jr. became upset. His father was in an unfamiliar mood. Then it dawned on him what Old Man Johnson had said just a short while ago about calling anytime.

Carl Jr. was stressed because he needed a phone, but the only one in the apartment was his mother's cell phone, which was on the table by the door. After telling Shakira and Michael to stay, he attempted to make his way to the phone without his father noticing him. Carl Jr. walked to the front of the house where his parents were and saw his father with his hand around his mother's neck.

He was choking her while yelling, "Do you hear me?! Huh?"

Carl's back was toward Carl Jr., so he didn't see him looking on while tiptoeing past. Quickly but quietly, Carl Jr. grabbed the phone, ran back into the room, and locked the door behind him. He then sat down in the closet with his brother and sister, who were now crying harder than they were before. Carl Jr. couldn't believe he had witnessed his father choking his mother.

Michael turned to his older brother and asked, "What happened? Why are you crying so much?"

"Nothing," Carl Jr. told him and then dialed Old Man Johnson's phone number.

On the first ring, he picked up the phone. "Hello, Barbara."

"No, Mr. Johnson. It's me, Carl Jr."

"What can I help you with?"

Before Carl Jr. could get one word out of his mouth, he heard his mother yell, "Get off of me! You're hurting me!"

When Carl Jr. grew silent, Old Man Johnson asked, "What, Carl Jr.? What's wrong?"

"My dad's choking my mother, and I can't do anything," Carl Jr. finally said, as he started to sob loudly.

Without another word, Old Man Johnson dropped the phone and ran up the stairs.

BAM! BAM! BAM!

"Open up!" Old Man Johnson shouted. "Open up in there! What's going on?"

All at once, the beating stopped and Carl went to the door.

"Why in the hell are you banging on my door?!" Carl screamed.

"I heard screaming and wanted to make sure everything was alright."

By that time, Michael, Shakira, and Carl Jr. had made their way around the corner. Old Man Johnson could see the tears in their eyes and the fear on their faces.

"Where is Mrs. Barbara?" he asked. "I need to speak with her."

"She's busy right now," Carl replied as he tried to slam the door, but Old Man Johnson proceeded to come in.

"I'm going to ask you one more time to speak to Mrs. Barbara." The look in his eyes was one that neither Carl nor the kids had ever seen before. It was cold, dark, and eerie, and gave Carl Jr. the chills.

Carl loosened his grip on the door immediately as if he had just seen a ghost.

Without turning around, Carl kept his eyes glued on Old Man Johnson as he gently yelled out, "Barbara...Barbara, someone's out here to see you."

Barbara took a minute to fix herself up and then made her way around the corner.

She smiled, holding in the pain and anger, and said, "What is it, Mr. Johnson?"

"Oh, nothing. I just thought I heard someone yelling, so I came up to make sure you and the kids were okay."

"Oh, we're fine. Everyone's okay up here, but thanks for checking on us."

Old Man Johnson looked around before looking back at Carl and saying, "I promised Barbara and the kids that I would never let anything happen to them as long as this old body of mine is still breathing."

12

He then turned around and walked back down the stairs.

After closing the door behind him, Carl looked at us in shame. He didn't know what he'd just done. Calmly, as if nothing had happened minutes prior to Old Man Johnson's arrival, Barbara turned to her children and told them to go do their homework while she prepared dinner. Carl Jr. was left feeling confused by how nonchalant his mother could act after such a big fight.

*****

It was two o'clock Saturday morning, and Carl had already left out, heading to his usual spot. When Carl Jr. got up to go to the bathroom, he heard a funny noise coming from his mother's room. Barbara always kept her door closed, but for some reason, it was open that night.

After Carl Jr. looked around to make sure his father was really gone, he crawled down the hall, slowly creeping until he reached his mother's door. He then placed his head against the door very gently, hoping not to be heard. That's when he could hear what was really going on, and he was crushed.

From the other side of the door, he heard his mother crying all over again, asking God to forgive Carl for his sins and to give her the strength to carry on. He sat there for hours listening to his mother squabble out her pain. She talked to God as if he were right there with her, telling God things Carl Jr. never knew.

That night, Carl Jr.'s life began to change. He promised himself that he would never tell anyone what he heard. He finally made his way back to his room, crying all over himself. Once back in his bed, he started his own conversation with the Lord.

Lord, why does my mother have to go through so much pain when she gives you so much glory? Why do we suffer when she works so hard? Why does Dad treat her so bad when she loves him so much? Why, Lord? Why, Lord? Why, Lord?

All night, Carl Jr. asked questions of WHY until he fell asleep.

CHAPTER 2

It was Saturday morning, and Carl Jr. was still in bed after being up all night talking to God. Michael woke him up by pulling the covers off him.

"Get up! Get up! It's almost eleven o'clock, and you're still sleeping."

"Leave me alone," Carl Jr. told his brother. "I've been up all night talking to God."

At that moment, Barbara was walking by their room. She stopped and looked at Carl Jr. as if to say she understood about him being tired since she had been up all night, conversing with God, also.

"Carl Jr., get up and get your brother and sister dressed. It's Saturday, and they want to go outside to play."

He pulled the covers back over his head, hoping for just a few more minutes of sleep.

"Carl Jr., what did I tell you to do?" he heard his mother say.

"Yes, ma'am," he replied with a sigh.

"Don't let me have to tell you again," Barbara warned.

"I'm up," he said, while rolling out of bed. "Michael, get what you want to put on so I can iron it."

"Here," said Michael. "This is what I'm wearing today."

"This? What do you mean, *this*?" Carl Jr. asked. "It doesn't match, Michael."

"Who says everything has to match all the time?" his brother replied.

Then, Carl Jr. thought to himself, *He's right. Mom and Dad don't always match.*

As they continued getting their stuff together, Shakira said to Carl Jr., "I don't need you to help me. I can get my own stuff together, and I can iron my own clothes."

Overhearing Shakira's conversation, Barbara rolled her neck around and yelled out, "Calm down, Ms. Grownie! I hear you in there. Carl Jr., I better not catch you letting Shakira touch that iron."

"Goodie for you," said Michael. "You're always running off at the mouth."

"At least I got one," said Shakira.

"What did I say? Don't let me come in there," their mother continued. "As a matter of fact, y'all hurry up and go outside before I change my mind."

Knock! Knock!

"Who is it?" Barbara called out.

"It's me…Little Reggie, Mrs. Henley."

Reggie lived on the other side of the projects where the Henley's had moved from not too long ago. He was the kind of kid no one wanted to have around, besides Carl Jr. Everyone thought Reggie was crazy, but Carl Jr. just thought Reggie was misunderstood, even though he did and said things sometimes that even shocked Carl Jr. So, from Reggie, Carl Jr. heard and saw it all. There wasn't too much Reggie could do to amaze Carl Jr. because he was always doing something. People use to always ask Carl Jr. why he would hung out with someone like Reggie and warned him that one day, Reggie would get him in a whole lot of trouble.

The way Reggie acted must not have bothered Carl Jr., though, because he and Reggie had been hanging since they were seven years old. Now at fourteen years old, Carl Jr. had known Reggie before he knew his own brother and sister.

"Come in and have a seat," Barbara told him. "They're in the back putting on their clothes. How's Mrs. Miller?" she asked.

"Okay," replied Reggie. "She had to have surgery last week. For what, I'm not really sure. When I asked, she told me to stay out of grown folk's business, but last night I overheard Taisa telling one of her girlfriends that Mom had something like breast cancer. Something about her titty getting cut off. I don't know."

"Reggie, don't say titty. That doesn't sound polite. It's called breast," Barbara corrected.

"What's breast, Mrs. Henley?

"Never mind, Reggie."

Reggie was twelve years old, but at times, he talked like he was seven or eight. That's one of the reasons why Carl Jr. hung around Reggie, because he felt Reggie needed him for guidance and protection. Michael didn't care for Reggie much, though. He hated the way Reggie played with Shakira and how he was always calling her names.

Finally, everyone was dressed and ready to hit the door. Shakira saw Reggie first.

"Hi, Reggie."

"Hey, ugly."

Michael immediately jumped in. "That's why no one likes you, Reggie, 'cause you're always running your big mouth."

"Be nice, Michael," Barbara intervened. "You know Reggie was just playing."

Barbara felt that something was wrong with Reggie, just as everyone else did, and that was the reason why many people let him get away with some of the little things.

"Everybody ready?" Carl Jr. yelled.

They all shouted in response, "Yeah."

Carl Jr. was the oldest of the bunch. Michael was six, and Shakira was only four and a half.

"Be careful, Carl Jr. Make sure you keep an eye on your brother and sister, as well as Reggie."

"Why Reggie?" asked Michael.

"Bye, Michael," Barbara said, ignoring his question.

Frowning, Michael closed the door behind him. Once they were gone, Barbara grabbed her cell phone and nervously called Mrs. Miller.

"Hello."

"Hi, Ann."

"Hey, Barbara."

Barbara didn't want to tell Ann what Reggie had said about her having cancer, because if she did, Ann would have worn Reggie's ass out. Ann didn't play. She was strict on her kids. They couldn't talk unless they were spoken to, and they couldn't eat but two times a day: breakfast and dinner.

Ann was a party girl, who loved the clubs, smoking, and drinking. She could come home after a hard day at work, pop the top on a can of Schlitz Malt Liquor, and light up a Newport at the same time. She thought just like men. Get a little bit and keep it moving.

Ann had two kids, Reggie and Taisa. Taisa was only eighteen, when she moved out of her mother's apartment and in with her boyfriend Brian, the neighborhood drug dealer. He was from uptown, or what people called, The Big Apple. Brian had all the little girls running behind him, but for some strange reason, Taisa had him hooked. Looking just like her mother, Taisa knew how to hook a man.

Barbara had been talking to Ann for about an hour, but Ann never mentioned anything about her cancer. She was getting antsy and about to rat Reggie out, when all of a sudden, Ann said, "Barbara, can I tell you something? You have to promise you'll keep it between us, though"

"I promise."

Ann repeated the question again. "Barbara, do you promise with all your heart that I won't ever hear this again, no matter what happens? Even if I'm on my deathbed."

Barbara paused before quietly responding, "I promise."

As Ann began to speak, her voice cracked, and she started crying before she could even say the first two words.

"Barbara, do you know my old ass has gone out here and gotten pregnant, and I didn't even know. Not only that, but when I went to the doctor last week, he told me that I have breast cancer and don't have long to live. The doctor told me if I choose to have this baby, I would live no longer than two weeks after it's born."

Barbara was speechless as Ann burst out in tears.

"Barbara, what am I going to do? How can I tell my kids that I'm pregnant and don't know who the father is? Or tell them that their mother doesn't have long to live. I'm damned if I do and damned if I don't. Who's going to look after my kids after I'm gone?"

"Where are their fathers?"

"Hell, I don't know their fathers. That's why I never kept a man around. I was too ashamed to say I didn't know which one I could call their father."

Ann went on for another hour crying and telling about all her other problems, until Barbara was at the point where she couldn't hear any more.

"Ann, I have to go now. The kids are outside, and I haven't heard from them in about three hours. I'll have to call you back later."

Before Barbara could hang up, Ann quickly said, "Thanks for being a friend. I knew you'd understand."

CHAPTER 3

Barbara went to the door after her long conversation with Ann, hoping to see the kids downstairs in the park. To her surprise, no one was around. She stood at the top of the stairs yelling their names one by one. First, she yelled for Shakira and Michael. Then she yelled Carl Jr.'s name, but still no answer.

Furious and at the same time scared, she made her way down the stairs. When she reached the bottom, she took a left around the building. Still, there were no kids in sight. Barbara made her way around the whole building, but didn't see them. That's when she started to panic, thinking and saying crazy things.

Did someone come and kidnap my kids? Did they follow someone to the store? All kinds of crazy things ran through Barbara's mind as she began to cry. *Should I call Carl and tell him that the kids are missing? Or should I call the police? No*, said the voice in Barbara's head. *Relax. Take a deep breath. Think. Think.*

Barbara sat down on the sidewalk by the park, hoping to see one of the kids come by, but an hour went by and there was still no sign of them. Scared to death, Barbara opened her cell phone and called Carl. Like always, there was no answer. This time, Barbara didn't leave a message.

Seeing the missed call, Carl called back immediately. "What is it? Why didn't you leave a message?"

"Carl, the kids have been missing for more than three hours and I can't find them anywhere," she replied, while bursting into tears.

"What did you say?"

Barbara repeated herself. "The kids are missing!"

Carl yelled, "Did you say you're cooking fried chicken?"

"Never mind." Barbara hung up the phone because Carl couldn't hear her from all the commotion going on in the background around him.

She finally got up, her eyes filled with tears, and headed back towards the stairs. When she noticed Old Man Johnson's chair was not on the porch, she knocked on the door, and there they were. All four of them were sitting on the floor, eating popcorn, and watching a Disney movie. Although angry, she smiled upon seeing that the kids were safe.

"Carl Jr.!" she yelled. "Didn't you hear me calling you? I've been looking for y'all for more than three hours, and y'all have been in here the whole time."

"Yes, Mother." Carl Jr. replied. "Mr. Johnson saw us on our way downstairs and asked if we wanted to come in to watch some movies, and we said yes."

Barbara walked over to Carl Jr., grabbed him by his shirt, and snatched him off the floor. She looked him in his eyes and said, "If you ever scare me like that again, I'm going to whip you so bad you won't be able to sit down for weeks."

Carl Jr. was petrified and shocked at the same time. He had never seen his mother this angry about any situation. Old Man Johnson saw Barbara's anger coming out and tried to calm her down.

"It's all my fault," said Old Man Johnson. "I should have told you that the kids were down here. I was just so happy to see them that the thought never crossed my mind. I'm sorry, Barbara. I promise you it won't ever happen again."

Barbara released her grip on Carl Jr.'s shirt, then told the kids to go upstairs to their rooms and not to come out. She made Reggie go home.

"Mrs. Henley, Mrs. Henley," Reggie said. "Is Carl Jr. going to get a beatin'?"

"No, Reggie, not this time."

"That's good, Mrs. Henley, because I love Carl Jr., and I don't want anyone to hurt him."

Reggie put his head down and walked towards the back of the building, while mumbling to himself, "Hurting Carl Jr. would make me mad, mad, mad."

Still stuck on thinking about what if something had happened to her children, Barbara never accepted Old Man Johnson's apology. However, she later calmed down and told the kids to come out the room. After sitting them down, she looked at the three of them and started crying all over again.

"I love y'all to death. Y'all are all I've got, and if something were to happen to y'all, it's no telling what I would do."

She hugged them as tight as she could and made them promise to never scare her like that again. Shakira was confused, but Michael and Carl Jr. knew what she meant. She was telling them how much she loved them.

Later that day, Barbara became upset with herself for having disrespected Old Man Johnson like that, and she felt that she owed him an apology.

Carl Jr. was sad for a long time after that day because he saw himself hurting his mother just like his daddy. He despised the fact that they even had the same name.

CHAPTER 4

After chatting over their favorite meal, that night ended lovely. However a little after one o'clock in the morning while everyone was sound asleep, there was a banging at the door.

BAM! BAM! BAM!

"Open up! It's me…Carl!"

"Hold on," Barbara yelled as she jumped out of her bed from a deep sleep.

BAM! BAM! BAM!

"Hurry, dammit! I got to use the bathroom!"

Barbara shouted, "I'm coming!"

She ran down the hallway with one arm in her nightgown and one bedroom shoe on her foot. She finally got to the door and opened it.

"Move, dammit!" Carl demanded, running past her while zipping his pants down. "Ahhh, yeah," he said as he pissed all over the toilet.

"What's wrong, Carl?" Barbara asked.

"Oh nothing. Just feeling good as hell."

"Well, must you be so loud? The kids are sleeping."

"Damn that! Where's the chicken you've been talking about?"

"I didn't say chicken. I was trying to tell you the kids were missing, but you were so busy getting drunk that you didn't hear a word I was saying."

"What in the hell do you mean the kids were missing? Weren't you watching them?"

"Yes, I was watching them."

"Well, how in the fuck did they go missing?"

"I *thought* they were missing. I found them hours later at Old Man Johnson's house watching movies."

Carl slammed the refrigerator door. "Why in the hell are my kids hanging out at that old pervert's house?"

"Be nice."

"I got your nice. That old man doesn't want me to go there with him, so you better tell him before I do," Carl warned.

"Tell him what?" she asked, not knowing what the big deal was all about.

"I don't want him around my fucking kids!"

"Carl, calm down. It's not that serious."

"Don't tell me any shit like that. For one, the old geezer never leaves his house. Two, he's always on that damn porch peeping at everyone that comes around. No one ever comes to visit him, and the fucker doesn't work. We've been on this side of the projects for over two years, and I've only heard him speak to me once. And he feels like he can come around here and talk to my wife and kids? I don't think so."

Barbara tried to speak, but Carl cut her off.

"I don't want to hear about Old Man Johnson no more, and if I do, there's going to be hell to pay."

Seeing that Carl was growing angrier, Barbara decided to let it go. "I'm going back to bed. I've got to get up early in the morning so I can get the kids ready for church."

"You and that damn church. That's why you never have any damn money. You're always giving it to that begging-ass preacher of yours."

"It's called tithes, Carl," she told him.

"Tides my ass. It's called pimpin' if you ask me, but you're too blind to see that. He got y'all niggas brainwashed. He's taking y'all money to buy a 500 Benz, rims, and big house, while we're catching cabs and packin' these projects like rats."

"Carl, I'm going to pray for you," Barbara said as she crawled back into bed.

"Don't pray for me, because your praying doesn't work. You've been praying all these years, and your black ass is in the same predicament I'm in. Ain't got shit and ain't gonna have shit."

Barbara fell back to sleep, leaving Carl up to carry on to himself. Michael and Shakira were sound asleep that night, but Carl Jr. was up thinking while looking out the window that faced the front of the building. With the apartment having thin walls, he could hear everything being said by his parents' bedroom, although his father was the only one still talking.

Carl finally went to sleep right where he sat, fully clothed and with his shoes. Since his father had quieted down, it wasn't long before Carl Jr. finally dozed off, too.

The next morning, Barbara entered the children's room. "Get up," she said. "Time to get up for church."

Carl Jr. was beat. It felt like he had just closed his eyes.

"Get up, Michael and Shakira. It's time to get ready."

Michael jumped up, grabbed his clothes, and brought back a matching outfit as if he knew Carl Jr. had been up all night thinking and didn't want to trouble him.

"Can you iron this for me?" Shakira asked as she walked out of the room.

Unbelievable. No mismatched clothes and no smart mouth from either of them, Carl Jr. thought to himself. For something like that to happen, he knew it had to be an act from God. After Carl Jr. finished getting dressed, he walked out the room to see his father still sitting in the same spot. Michael and Shakira stood over him in disbelief.

Shakira yelled out, "Mommy! Mommy! Why are Dad's pants wet in the front and smell like pee?"

"That's not pee, dummy. Dad just spilt something on himself," Michael said.

"Why would you say something like that, Shakira?" Barbara asked.

Carl Jr. never commented because he knew Shakira was right. Their father had laid there during the night and peed all over himself. Barbara looked at Carl Jr. in shame as she wiped the tears from her eyes.

"Shakira, Michael, let's go. I don't want to be late for church. Y'all know how y'all get when everyone turns around to stare because someone walked in church late."

Their mother turned off all the lights and told Carl Jr. to lock the door behind him since he was the last one to exit the apartment. They then made their way downstairs to see Old Man Johnson sitting in his usual spot.

"Hi, Mrs. Henley."

"Hey, Mr. Johnson."

"I see you and the kids are heading out to church."

"Oh yeah, I've got to give the Lord his time." Barbara never stopped walking as she made her way to the cab, holding tight to Shakira and Michael.

Old Man Johnson was lost, thinking to himself that she was acting a bit strange. Carl Jr. knew what was wrong, though, and because he really liked Old Man Johnson and the way he looked out for them, he felt he had to find a way to tell him what his father had said.

So, he played it off and told his mother that he had to go back to make sure he had locked the door. Once he got to the bottom of the stairs, he talked to Old Man Johnson from afar, telling all the mean things his father had said about him, which would explain why his mother was acting the way she was. Old Man Johnson never said a word as he sat there in his chair looking like he had just lost his best friend.

"Carl Jr., bring your butt on!" Barbara yelled in an angry tone.

"Bye, Mr. Johnson. I have to go now before Mother kills me."

He put his hand up and waved goodbye, but never said a word. Carl Jr. was hurt because he could see the pain in Old Man Johnson's eyes. When he finally got in the cab, he slammed the door and looked out the window, while hiding his anger and tears for his friend, Old Man Johnson.

CHAPTER 5

"Stop right here," Barbara told the cab driver. "We'll walk from here."

The kids got out ashamed when the cab pulled up in front of the church.

"Anything for you, Mrs. Henley," said Joe, the cab driver.

"Thanks a bunch," she replied, while reaching into her purse for money to pay him.

"No, no, no. Put that away. This one's on me."

Barbara still reached out to hand him the money. "You have to get paid for your services."

Joe pushed her hand away. "Sometimes just being able to help someone else is worth more than money. It's a blessing."

Smiling at Joe, she put the money back into her purse and thanked him once again.

"One-thirty, same spot, Mrs. Henley?"

"Yes, Joe, same spot, and don't be late."

"Oh, I won't," he said. "You don't have to worry about that."

*****

"Good morning, Sister Henley."

"Good morning, Sister Jones. Looks like a full house today."

"Oh yeah, Pastor's got visitors from Saint Calvary First Baptist Church coming in."

"Coming from where?"

"Girl, all the way from Montgomery, Alabama. I heard they have one of the baddest choirs in the whole state of Alabama."

Barbara didn't reply because she knew if she did, Sister Jones would go on rambling for days about nothing. Sister Jones had always been that way.

It was the middle of service, and Carl Jr. had to use the bathroom really bad since he had forgotten to go before they left home. He sat there for a while trying to hold it in, but he couldn't. After looking around to see who was looking, he worked his way to the back. His leaving the sanctuary was just as bad as coming into church late. Everyone started turning around.

"Hey, you. Hey," Sister Jones said. "Where do you think you're going?"

"To the restroom."

"Don't you see the preacher's preaching?"

"Yes, ma'am, I do, Carl Jr. replied. "But I have to go real bad. I've been holding this since I left the house."

"No excuses," said Sister Jones. "Go have a seat and learn to have some respect."

Carl Jr. stood there confused, holding his stomach as tight as he could to keep from using the bathroom on himself.

"Go, I said. Go sit down," Sister Jones told him.

Trembling, he was ready to give her a piece of his mind, but all he could hear was my mother's voice in his head: *Carl Jr., you better not ever let me hear you disrespecting grown folks no matter what they say. Because if you do, it will be the last time you sit down straight.*

After looking up at Sister Jones with a hateful look on my face, he made his way back to his seat. A few minutes later, urine saturated his pants, and Barbara was furious.

Looking straight ahead, she said, "Don't tell me you just used the bathroom in your pants."

"Yes, ma'am," he whispered in response.

Barbara never said another word. She just grabbed her son by the wrist and pulled him down the aisle.

"Up again?" said Sister Jones.

Barbara pulled Carl Jr. past her without uttering a reply.

"Carl Jr., what were you thinking? Why did you go to the bathroom on yourself?"

Before he could explain, his mother yelled out, "You're gonna be just like that old father of yours! Trifling and good for nothing. How could you just sit there and use the bathroom on yourself? What kind of man does that but your father?"

After Barbara finished scolding Carl Jr., she told him to go stand outside by the old oak tree on the side of the church and not to move until service was over. Doing as he was told, he stood by the tree crying his eyes out. Not because he had wet his pants, but because his mother was disappointed in him and had said he would turn out to be like his no-good father, which is a person he definitely didn't want to be.

An hour went by, and Joe, the cab driver, pulled up thirty minutes before church let out to see Carl Jr. still standing there crying. He got out, walked over, and asked him what was wrong. Carl Jr. commenced to tell him what happened, and after he finished, Joe sat down on the ground by the tree and began telling Carl Jr. about himself when he was his age.

Carl Jr. couldn't believe what he was hearing. Every time he saw Joe, he was always smiling and telling people how good God was to him, and how happy he was to be who he was. But, in reality, Joe had it rough growing up. He told Carl Jr. about when he was just nine years old; his dad left them and never came back. Never called or nothing. Joe said his mother went into a state of depression, losing her mind, and was admitted into a mental hospital. He said he was later sent to a foster home, where he soon got new parents.

Everything was good, until one day when Joe's foster father came home drunk and started beating on his foster mother, blaming her for not being able to have kids. He said she screwed up his life and he wished he'd never met her. On top of those hurtful words, his foster father used to always remind Joe that he wasn't blood.

"They said my parents left me because I wasn't shit, and that I was going to grow up and never change."

Carl Jr. could see the tears building up in Joe's eyes as he went on telling his life story.

"There were many days and nights where I just wanted to kill myself. I asked the Lord why? Why did He bring me there to suffer like that?"

It wasn't long before Joe started crying and wiping tears from his eyes.

Joe looked up at him and said, "Carl Jr., my life has been hell for a long time, until one day my foster father came home drunk, like always. But, this time, he was in a different type of mood. I remember that day like it was yesterday. He came into my room and told me that he was going to see me in Hell because I was the devil, put on this earth to seek and destroy happy families, and that one day, I was going to get what was coming to me. He then slammed the door, went into the room with my foster mother, and started blaming her for adopting me and for convincing him it was okay not to have a child of their own.

"That's when it all changed. All I heard was POW...POW...POW! And then my foster father started calling out to the Lord, asking him why. 'Why me, Lord?' he had said. That's when I heard one more POW! Then everything went silent. I couldn't believe what I was hearing, so I waited for about twenty minutes before going into their bedroom. There they both were lay side by side in a pool of blood. I was devastated for many years after that, but I had a change of heart about dying and realized living was a wonderful thing. Despite all the evil that goes on, you have to make the best of what you have and trust that the Lord will see you through.

"Enough of that," said Joe. "I've got to get myself together. I don't want your mother to see my crying like this."

Carl Jr. stopped crying, as well, and suddenly, he was happy all over again because Joe made him realize he wasn't the only one going through things and that some people had it worse than he did.

Like always, Barbara, Shakira, and Michael came out to the cab on time.

"How was church?" Joe asked.

"Oh, fine," Barbara replied, while not bothering to look at her oldest son. Once inside the cab, she finally spoke to Carl Jr. and said, "You and I have some talking to do."

During the ride home, everyone was silent, not knowing what was going to happen next. Then, all of a sudden, Joe spoke out.

"Mrs. Henley, mind if I share something with you without you getting upset?"

"Of course," she replied.

Joe approached the subject carefully. "Well, you know your kids are the most respectful kids I have ever met. They look up to you like no other. They instill the things you say and exercise those things to the fullest, knowing that if they did anything other than what you have taught them it would be unacceptable."

Barbara smiled. "Thanks, Joe. I try my hardest to be the best mother and father I can be."

Joe paused for a second before continuing. "I know it's none of my business, but I can't stand to see someone blamed for something that really wasn't their fault." He then took his eyes off the road for a moment to look Barbara in her eyes. "Believe me, I know just how that feels. It's been that way for me most of my life. And today, I saw something happen to an innocent young man who was just doing what his mother told him to do."

"What are you getting at, Joe?"

"Carl Jr. told me what happened in church today and that you never gave him a chance to explain. You said things to him that really hurt his feelings."

Barbara cut Joe off. "He knows what he did. He needed to get his feelings hurt."

"Let me finish," he said. "If you would have heard him out, you wouldn't be saying that. It was Sister Jones that made him go back to his seat after he told her over and over how bad he had to go to the restroom. She still insisted that he go sit down and told him that he needed to have some respect. That's why Carl Jr. returned to his seat. Not because she told him, but because he remembered what you told him years ago about disrespecting a grown person and that you would whip him until he couldn't sit down."

Barbara sat there for a minute, staring out the window without saying a word. Then she turned around with her hand over her mouth and tears rolling down her face. While looking at her oldest son, she apologized for not allowing him to explain and for telling him that he was going to turn out to be just like his father.

Carl Jr. was speechless, just like he always was whenever his mother cried, no matter what she was crying for. He knew if she was crying, she was hurting, and that's something he didn't want her to do.

Joe jumped in. "So, Mrs. Henley, now that that's all cleared up, I think it's time for a celebration. How about some ice cream for everyone?"

"Yeah, yeah, yeah!" shouted Michael and Shakira, while jumping up and down in the backseat of the cab.

"Joe, we can't."

"Why not?"

"I don't have money for that, although it sounds nice."

"Oh, no. This one is on me. You just sit back and relax for a change."

Barbara looked back at her children and saw how excited they were. "Okay. It's ice cream for everyone."

It was like the happiest day of their lives. Barbara was smiling and relaxed, free from everything for one time in her life.

CHAPTER 6

"Oh my God! We have to go. It's been almost three hours since we left church, and I haven't cooked or nothing. Carl is going to kill me," Barbara said.

Joe looked at her with a bit of disappointment and then told the children to load up. "Maybe one day we can do this again."

The kids were still amped up, bouncing around in the backseat while singing, "We had some ice cream! We had some ice cream!"

However, as they got closer to the house, the darker things got and the quieter Barbara became. Finally, the cab pulled up to the front of the building after the long, but short ride, and they were back in the hood again.

"Thanks, Joe," Barbara said. "We really had a wonderful time today, and who knows, maybe we'll do this again someday."

"Anytime, Mrs. Henley. Anytime."

As Joe drove off, the children yelled goodbye and then made their way to the house.

"Hello, kids," said Old Man Johnson, sitting in his usual spot as he read the Sunday newspaper.

"Hey, Mr. Johnson," they replied.

Shakira yelled out, "We had ice cream! We had ice cream!"

Then Barbara said, "Yeah, Joe, the cab driver, took us to this place that had rides, games, and everything. The kids and I had a ball."

"Oh yeah?" said Old Man Johnson.

"Yes," she replied. "Go upstairs, kids."

"Glad to see you and the kids are getting out and having a little bit of fun."

"Oh, it was nice to see them singing and playing like that. It really made my day. I'll talk to you later. I have to get up here and cook this old man of mine something to eat."

"'Til next time, Mrs. Henley."

Barbara made her way upstairs, opened the door, and saw Carl standing there with a grim look on his face. Holding a ham sandwich in his hand, he yelled out to her, "Where in the hell have y'all been all this time?"

"I'm sorry," she said. "I didn't realize we'd been gone so long. Time just flew by."

"Flew by my ass. I've been sitting here all morning starving my ass off while you and the kids were running around and bullshitting."

"No one was bs'ing, Carl. I took the kids out for some ice cream and let them run around the park for a while."

"Ice cream? Ice cream! You mean to tell me that you had me up here starving while you and the kids were playing games and eatin' ice cream. Are you crazy?"

"No, I'm not crazy."

"You must be. Besides, you told me you didn't have any money."

"And I didn't. Joe paid for it," she informed him.

"Who the fuck is Joe?"

"The cab driver, the one who takes us to church every Sunday morning."

Carl paused, reached back his hand, then hauled off and slapped her as hard as he could across her face. Barbara didn't say a word as she picked herself off the floor.

"Get up, dammit! Before I put my foot somewhere it doesn't belong."

He then grabbed her by the neck and slammed her against the refrigerator. "Next time you tell me that another man took you anywhere, I'm going to mop the floor with your head."

Carl Jr. stood there speechless, but Michael and Shakira were crying their eyes out because it was the first time they had ever seen their father hit her like that.

"Carl, please," Barbara pleaded. "The kids are looking."

"Let them look. Maybe they might learn something."

"Carl, please. I'm begging you to stop it. Stop it! Let me go!"

Out of nowhere, Shakira ran over and hit him with an old elephant ornament from off the coffee table. "Stop, Daddy! Stop, Daddy! Stop hitting Mother."

Before you knew it, Carl had Shakira up in the air by her shirt.

"Put her down!" Barbara demanded. "Not my damn kids," she screamed while grabbing Carl by the arm.

Carl Jr. was lost for real. His mother had just said a curse word, and he knew it was on then.

Michael ran up to his father and hit him with the broom. "Get off my mother!"

All Carl Jr. could do was stand there staring and lost. He was in a deep daze, having flashbacks of all the times he had seen his father be mean to his mother, but he didn't do anything.

Knock! Knock!

Carl Jr. ran as fast as he could to the door because he knew it was Old Man Johnson coming to save the day. However, when he opened the door, he immediately saw it wasn't Old Man Johnson; it was his best friend Reggie.

"What's going on?" Reggie asked when he saw the tears falling from his friend's eyes.

Before Carl Jr. could reply, Reggie saw Mr. Henley in action. Reggie went into a rage that Carl Jr. had never seen him in before. He grabbed a can of Lysol and sprayed it in Mr. Henley's face. Next, Reggie hauled off and kicked him in his privates, and then commenced to beat him in the head with the can.

"Stop, stop, stop, Reggie!" Barbara yelled as she pulled Michael and Shakira away.

It was like Reggie couldn't even hear her telling him to stop. It was like he had zoned out. Mr. Henley was out a long time before, but Reggie kept beating him.

"Stop him!" Barbara shouted. "Stop him, Carl Jr.!"

In his mind, Carl Jr. didn't want him to stop, but he had to do what his mother said.

"Stop, Reggie," Carl Jr. told his friend in a soft voice.

It was like Reggie couldn't hear anyone's voice but his friend's. Barbara was happy and pissed off at the same time.

"Go home, Reggie, and don't come back until I say you can."

"No one hurts Carl Jr. No one, Mrs. Henley," Reggie said before walking out the door.

That Sunday was the craziest day of Carl Jr.'s life. He learned two important things that day: his mother really did love her children like she said, and Reggie loved him even more.

That night was a quiet night because no one knew what Carl was thinking after what Reggie had done to him.

CHAPTER 7

It was Monday morning around five-fifteen, when Carl finally woke up. He had a big knot on the top of his head and his privates were hurting from the intense beating Reggie had put on him.

"Barbara, can you get me an icepack and some Tylenol for this excruciating pain."

"Of course," she said, while smiling inside.

"Daddy, are you okay?" Shakira asked.

"Yes, sweetie. Daddy's just hurting a bit."

Michael never said anything. Instead, he just looked at Carl in disbelief. As for Carl Jr., it was one of the happiest days of his life. Someone had finally given his father what he had coming for a long time…a beating.

The children continued getting dressed for school while their father lay in bed all morning, moaning and groaning from the intense beating.

"Okay, kids, off to school," said Barbara. As they walked out the door, their mother gave each of them a big hug and a kiss. "I love you very much," she told them.

"Bye, kids. Hope you have a good day," said Carl.

It was the first time in years they'd heard him talk like that, and they were all speechless while making their way downstairs to the bus stop.

"Good morning, kids," said Old Man Johnson as he read the paper.

The children spoke back and continued walking.

"Hey, Carl Jr., when you get back from school, stop by. I have something to give you."

"Yes, sir, I will," Carl Jr. replied.

That day at school went lovely. It was like the old days when they looked forward to coming home. The school day went by fast, and before they knew it, they were on their way home.

"Hey, Carl Jr., guess what happened to me today at school," said Michael.

"What?"

"I got an A on my math test, and the teacher let me go in front of the class to show how I worked out my problem. It felt good. Now I know what I'm going to be when I grow up."

"And what's that?" Carl Jr. asked.

"A teacher," Michael replied. "A college professor."

Carl Jr. looked at Michael. "Anything's possible as long as you work hard for it."

Michael and his older brother continued to talk all the way home.

"Okay, kids. This is your stop," the bus driver announced.

After running to the front of the bus, they jumped off the second step.

"Last one to the house is a rotten egg," said Michael.

Like always, Michael got to the step first. He knew he could outrun Carl Jr., which is why he would call that game. As they walked up the stairs, Old Man Johnson came out and called for Carl Jr.

"Carl Jr., did you forget to stop by? I told you that I have something for you."

"Oh man, I sure did," he said, while turning back around.

Old Man Johnson went into the back room and came out with a little brown box.

"In this box is a gift from my great-grandfather passed down for many generations, but I thought it would stop here because I have no one to give it to. That's when I thought about you."

He stared Carl Jr. dead in his eyes. "I see you as my child, and pray that one day I will be able to raise you like I would have raised my own."

Once again, Carl Jr. was speechless and just watched as Old Man Johnson placed the box on the table.

"This box is not to be opened until the day I die." He then stuck his hand in his shirt pocket and handed Carl Jr. a tiny key. "Guard this key with all your life. This is the only key I have that will open the box. If you lose this key, you will never open the box. And if you do open this box without the key, you will be haunted by all those who've passed and have opened the box before you."

Carl Jr. looked at Old Man Johnson with a fearful expression and said, "I'm scared. I don't want the key."

"Open your hand, Carl Jr.," he said, placing the key in the palm of his hand. "Don't worry. I know you're the one that will hang on to this key and pass it down to your kids. I will let you know the box's location when I'm on my dying bed."

"What's in the box, Mr. Johnson?" he asked.

"That's never to be told. Only the one with the key will know what's in it, and he has to open it himself."

After accepting the key, Carl Jr. started to make his way upstairs. However, before he left, Old Man Johnson told him, "This secret is between the two of us. No one else needs to know, not even your mother."

He even made Carl Jr. promise to never tell.

That night, Carl Jr. tossed and turned until the late hours of the night, trying to figure out what was inside the box. He thought it was strange Old Man Johnson would choose him out of all the people that he came in contact with during his life.

For weeks, Carl Jr. tried to make sense out of the whole thing concerning the box, until he finally gave up and just started protecting the key. On a brighter note, things were better in the Henley household. Carl had been staying home at night. Michael and Shakira were getting along, and Barbara was finally getting the rest she needed.

CHAPTER 8

Three weeks had gone by, and all was well until Saturday around two o'clock in the morning. Barbara's phone had been ringing off the hook. She didn't answer it the first few times because she didn't recognize the number and thought maybe someone had the wrong number.

Finally, she picked up. "Hello."

"Hi, Mrs. Henley. This is Taisa, Reggie's sister."

"Oh, hi, Taisa. What's wrong? Did something happen to your mother?"

Taisa paused for a moment. "No, Mrs. Henley. It's Mr. Henley. Somehow he got himself in a bit of trouble at Joe's Poker Shack, and I had to bring him home."

"What kind of trouble?" Barbara asked.

"I promised not to tell, Mrs. Henley. But, he's okay now, just a bit drunk. He said he doesn't want the kids to see him like that anymore. Don't worry, Mrs. Henley. I called my mother and asked if he can sleep on the couch until he gets himself together. She said it was fine and told me to call to let you know what had happened."

"Thanks a lot," Barbara told her, then hung up.

"Who was that, Mother?" Carl Jr. asked, coming into the room after being awakened by the ringing phone.

"Oh, nobody important. Just someone asking about your father."

"Is he okay?"

"Oh yeah, he's just fine. Go to bed and get some sleep."

Carl Jr. made his way back to bed, but even after several hours went by, he still couldn't get back to sleep because he knew his father had gotten into something.

That morning, while getting ready for school, Shakira noticed her father wasn't there.

"Mommy, where's Daddy?"

"Oh, he had to leave early this morning to check on a new job."

"A new job?" Michael said. "Dad is getting a new job?"

"Yes, Michael. He's trying."

Immediately, Carl Jr. knew something was really wrong because Barbara never lied to her children.

"Carl Jr., where do you think you're going without your brother and sister?"

He never answered; he just stood by the door frowning as he waited on them.

"Goodbye, kids. Have a good day," Barbara said as they walked out the door.

"Good morning, kids," said Old Man Johnson. "Hey, Carl Jr., is everything okay?"

"Yes, sir. Everything's fine."

"So why do you have that sad look on your face?"

"Oh, nothing. Just tired from being up all night."

"Not good, my friend," Old Man Johnson told him. "I know there's something that's keeping you up. Stop by after school so we can talk about it."

"Okay, Mr. Johnson," he replied as he made his way to the bus stop.

"What's up, Carl Jr.?"

"Hey, Reggie."

"Carl Jr., why do you look so sad?"

"I'm not sad, just tired. I've been up all night."

"Yeah, me too."

"What kept you up all night?" Carl Jr. asked his friend.

"It was because Taisa brought your dad to sleep on the couch because he was too drunk to go home. He snored like a bear all night."

Again, this was another time that Carl Jr. was speechless. "Who else knows this, Reggie?" he finally asked.

"No one. Just me, you, my sister, and my mother."

"Good. Let this be our little secret."

That day went by slow. It was like someone or something had slowed down the hands of time. Finally, school was out, and Carl Jr. was on his way home, eager to see Old Man Johnson so he could tell him what his friend had told him.

"Hello, Mr. Johnson."

"Hi, Carl Jr."

"Mind if we go in?"

"No, my son. After you."

Carl Jr. entered Old Man Johnson's apartment and sat by the door so he could hear if someone was calling for him.

"So, young man, what's on your little mind?"

He looked around for a second and then began to tell his story. He shared with Old Man Johnson what he heard last night and what Reggie had told him that morning. Once Carl Jr. finished, Old Man Johnson sat down in a chair beside him and began to share things he knew about the Henley family. Carl Jr. had no idea he knew so much about them.

"Carl Jr., I sit out here all day and night because I can't sleep. I see and hear everything that goes on around here. I just don't say anything. I know things about your father that I wish not to discuss, and I pray every day that he doesn't come home and harm any of you."

"Why is my dad so cruel? Why doesn't he love us like a father should? We're not bad kids. Mother's not a bad wife, and she loves him with all her heart."

"I don't know," replied Old Man Johnson. "Sometimes I ask myself the same question. Look at me. I'm just a troubled old man living day-by-day, with really no reason to carry on. It gets lonely down here, Carl Jr., real lonely. That's why I'm always sitting out here on the porch reading papers. Ever since my family passed, I've been the same. No matter how hard I try, still 'til this day, I ask the Lord why. What did I do wrong to deserve to have my whole family taken from me? Who did I hurt to have to suffer all these years? Still, I have no answer."

"Do you believe in God, Mr. Johnson?"

"Yes, Carl Jr., I do."

"Then why does God let us suffer this way? Mother says all you have to do is have faith and God will see you through."

"I have faith, Carl Jr. That's why I think I lived this way for so long, because God's going to bless me with the family I always dreamed of."

"Me, too, Mr. Johnson. God's going to bless me with the father I've been dreaming of for all these years; a father that doesn't drink and beat on his wife. One who doesn't stay out all night and loves his kids the way a father's supposed to."

"Don't worry, Carl Jr., one day that old father of yours is going to leave and never come back. You and your family are going to live that life you've been dreaming about."

"For real, Johnson! Do you think the Lord will bless us like that?" Carl Jr. asked, sounding excited about the possibility of it happening.

"Yes, my son, I really do. All you have to do is keep the faith like your mother says, and everything will be alright."

"Thanks, Johnson. I really needed to hear that. Now I know one day me and my family are going to live and act like a normal family with another father."

"One day, my son, one day."

"Carl Jr.! Carl, Jr., where are you?" Michael yelled from the top of the stairs.

"Got to go, Mr. Johnson. I've got to help them with their homework before Mother gets home."

As Carl Jr. stood to make his way to the door, Old Man Johnson hugged him and said, "I'm always here for you, and I'll do anything you ask."

"Thanks again," Carl Jr. replied, then continued out the door and up the stairs.

CHAPTER 9

It was time for Barbara to come home and everything was on point. That is until Carl walked in.

"Hey, kids. How was yawls' day?"

"It was good," Michael responded. "It's just I have been working extra hard at my grades because I'm going to be a college professor when I grow up."

"Oh, yeah?" said Carl.

"Yeah, so I can take care of my family like you. Mother told us that you had a new job you were going to check on and that's why you had to leave at four o'clock this morning."

Carl hesitated for a second. "Oh…oh, yeah. That interview didn't go so good. I didn't get the job."

"Don't worry," said Michael. "You'll get the job you've been wanting. You just have to keep trying at it."

Carl Jr. didn't say anything because he knew his father was lying.

Barbara soon walked through the door. "Hey, kids."

"Hi, Mom," the children greeted in unison.

"How was yawls' day?"

"Good," they replied.

"Homework done yet?"

"Yes, ma'am," they all said at once.

Barbara didn't know Carl was home because she never made it to the back room, and he never came out. Before doing anything, she always came home and went straight to the kitchen to cook dinner.

"Daddy didn't get the job, but I told him to keep trying," said Michael.

Barbara didn't comment because she knew the whole job thing was a lie. Carl Jr. could see the pain and anger on his mother's face. It killed her to have to lie to her children, and at that time, Carl was getting on her last nerve.

"Hey, baby," Carl said as he made his way back to the front.

"Hey, Carl."

"What's that you're cooking? It smells great."

Barbara never answered. Carl knew she was pissed, so he played it off and looked in the pot himself.

"Oh, that looks good, but not as good as my lovely wife."

Still, she didn't comment. Carl finally got the hint and left her alone.

"Can we go out and play for a little?" Shakira asked.

"Yes," Barbara replied, "but don't go too far because dinner will be ready soon."

After they grabbed their things and were out the door, Carl Jr. said, "Go ahead, Michael and Shakira. I'm gonna sit here on the step for a minute and wait for Reggie."

"Okay," said Michael, "but don't take all day, because you know we don't have long."

"I won't, Michael."

Carl Jr. sat on the steps waiting for the worse. In his heart, he knew once he and his siblings left out the apartment, Carl was going to give his mother hell for not answering him. Sure enough, it wasn't a minute later when Carl began.

"What's wrong with you, lady? I know you heard me talking to you."

Barbara still didn't answer.

"Don't get smacked up in here. I ain't in the mood for that right now. I've been out all night, and I'm tired as hell."

She finally spoke. "I bet you are. Carl, what's gotten into you? For the last few years, you've been acting like a madman, and every year it gets worse."

"Woman, you trippin'!"

"No, Carl, you trippin'. Every week it's something new with you. What's next week?"

"Barbara, why you always bitching about nothing?"

"What do you call nothing, Carl? Is not having a real job anything? Is not helping with the bills anything? Is not spending time with your kids anything? Oh my bad, Carl, I guess you're right. When it comes down to those things, you ain't doing nothing."

Carl jumped in. "Hold your horses, lady. You better mind how you talk to me. I might not be the man you want me to be, but I'm still the man of this damn house."

"What house, Carl? You call this a house? A three-bedroom apartment in an overcrowded project with more problems than a little bit. You think I want my kids growing up like this? Having to bathe together because the water gets cold so fast. Having to sleep together because there ain't enough room. Not being able to sleep good at night because of all the gang violence and police sirens. No, Carl. And no, this is not our home."

"Don't blame me for this shit. You're the one giving all your money to that old pastor of yours."

"Is that all you can say, Carl? I get so tired of that same ol' line. Be a man, Carl. Learn to be a better father to your kids. Can you do that?"

"I am a father, and a damn good one at that."

"You call staying out all night, getting drunk, and having to sleep at the neighbor's house because you were too embarrassed to come home being a good father? I don't think so, buddy."

Carl Jr. sat there for about an hour listening to them go back and forth, knowing eventually his father was going to get mad and act out.

Sure enough, Carl yelled out, "That's enough, dammit! Don't say another word. Now, I have sat here for more than an hour listening to you tell me how sorry of a man I am, but did you take the time out to ask what made me like that? You're right. I was that hard-working man, that loving husband, and that good father to his children. But, all that changed when the lady that I met went from one hundred and twenty pounds with long black hair to one hundred and ninety pounds with short brown hair. I changed once the money I was making stopped going a long way. Then came two more damn kids, and now my money ain't shit. You're right. I changed. I ain't the man I used to be. Thanks to you and all those damn kids, I'm never gonna get ahead."

Barbara was silent, and so was Carl Jr. who sat outside overhearing everything. His heart sped up, and he felt a cold chill run through his body while a warm tear rolled down his face. *Lord, what just happened?* he thought. *Why did I have to hear what I just heard? My father, my own flesh and blood, blames his downfall on his wife and kids.*

Barbara waited for a while and then spoke to Carl in a low clear voice. "Carl, I loved you then like I do now, no matter how much you gain or how much money you make. Even though the past few years have been a living hell for me and my kids, I still love you like I did the day I married you."

She continued. "Carl, I stood before God and promised him that I would love you 'til death do us part, no matter what the case may be. Not even the beating and swearing you lay upon me will make me fail my God. But, for you to stand here and blame the kids and I for your worldly mistakes is absurd. That's one of the most hurtful things a man can say to his wife about his own kids. The devil's a liar, and I should not give him the glory, for this battle has not been won. I'm gonna pray for you, Carl, and ask God to spare you, for you know not what you do."

Carl jumped in. "See, that's the shit I'm talking about right there. Every time shit doesn't go right, you go running to God. Obviously, the man doesn't hear you. The shit I'm dealing with is right here, right now. And I'm not depending on some man or ghost to solve them. That's what's wrong with you tired women. Always depending on *the man* to bail y'all out. I think that's why God was created in the first place. Some tired-ass woman needed someone to cry to that she knew couldn't speak back. That way, she could tell and answer her own damn questions."

Barbara didn't say another word. Soon, Carl Jr. heard her slam her bedroom door as hard as she could. Like many other days, that was the worst day of Carl Jr.'s life. He was left feeling confused. What man, or father, would be so cruel and bitter towards living and life itself?

CHAPTER 10

After that day, things were a bit quiet around the house. Carl either felt a little guilty for some of the bad things he had said to Barbara, or maybe he was really trying to change. Weeks went by, and Carl never left the house. Carl Jr. noticed the change in his father and began to think something was wrong. So did, Barbara, but they both knew better than to say anything.

It wasn't long before Carl started getting antsy and agitated about being in the house. He started making five-second phone calls but never said anything to the person on the other end. He would just listen as the person said hello and asked him to stop playing on the phone. No one noticed it at first except Carl Jr., but it soon became too obvious. It seemed like not an hour passed that he wasn't making that same phone call.

Barbara finally got pissed. "Whoever you're calling so much, you might need to go see them."

"Stay out my damn business and don't worry about who I'm calling," Carl replied.

"I can't help but be in your business, when you're sitting right in front of me acting like a two-year-old with a new toy."

Carl never responded. He just sat there staring at his cell phone. Barbara left it alone after that and carried on like usual.

It was around 1:30 a.m. that Friday night, when Carl Jr. got up to use the restroom and noticed his father was gone. After he returned to his bedroom, he opened his window so he could hear when or if his father came home. Thirty minutes went by, and he finally started getting sleepy. That's when he heard his father's voice.

"Hey, Old Man Johnson. You got nothing else better to do than to sit here all night watching who comes and goes."

Old Man Johnson replied, "Carl, one day, you're going to be worth something to those kids and their mother."

"I done told you one time, old man, to stay out my family business."

"What family business? You think I don't know what you've been up to?"

"You don't know shit about me, old man."

"Oh, you don't think I know you've been beating on Barbara and taking her money down to Joe's Poker Shack tricking with those young girls? You don't think I know you spend your whole check getting high on those drugs? You don't think I know you've been seeing someone else these past few years? I thought so. I know more than you think I know."

By then, Carl Jr. was wide awake with his ear closer to the window so he wouldn't miss a thing.

"Let me tell you something, old man, and I'm only going to tell you this once. If you ever mention any of this shit to my wife, it'll be the last time you tell someone else's business."

Old Man Johnson replied, "Are you threatening me, boy? Is that what I'm hearing?"

"That's not a threat. It's a promise."

Carl turned around to head up the stairs, but before he could get his foot on the first step, Old Man Johnson grabbed him from behind and put him in a chokehold. Old Man Johnson spoke to Carl in a calm, cold voice.

"If you think for a minute that I wouldn't cut your throat and think nothing of it, then try me, punk boy. You ain't no damn man. That's why you come home and beat on your wife, because you scared to hit a man. Nigga, I can see right through you.

"I heard what you said about me sitting out here all day and night being in other people's business, and that I don't have no life. Well, you're right about me not having a life. I lost mine many years ago to a truck driver, and I've been feeling guilty ever since. I found that truck driver and followed him for many years until I made my move. I took his family's life like he took mine--one by one until they were all dead. Now, I have to live with that for the rest of my life. I sit out here all day and night to keep from having to kill someone else. Someone like you who has a good family and kids to raise but wants to throw it all away for the streets. So, the next time you feel like threatening someone, know who you're talking to."

Old Man Johnson turned Carl loose and threw him to the ground. Carl lay there for a minute gasping for air, trying to get his breath back and scared out of his mind, while Old Man Johnson went in the house and closed the door. Carl soon made his way in the house to lay down on the couch without saying a word to anyone.

Carl Jr. stayed up all night replaying in his head what he had seen and heard. He was devastated to learn that the old man who lived underneath his family was a stone cold killer. On top of that, he learned that his father was on drugs.

*****

Months went by with things being the same as always, but this particular day, Barbara spoke out because Carl had spent the rent money gambling down at Joe's Poker Shack, knowing he was already a month behind.

"Get out!" she screamed. "Get your things and get out! I can't do this anymore. I tried to love you. I tried to make it work, but it seems the harder I try, the worse things get. I asked the Lord to make me strong. I asked the Lord to change your ways, but it still seems like a no-win situation."

"Stop crying about nothing," Carl responded nonchalantly. "I'm going to get the rent paid."

"Carl, you said that last month, and this month, it's the same thing."

"Please, woman, stop stressing me. I told you that I was gonna get it paid."

"No, Carl, I don't want you to get it paid. I just want you to leave."

"You can't pay these damn bills by yourself."

"Why not? I've been doing it all this time," she shot back.

"Say what you want, but I'm not going no damn where."

Barbara sat down, grabbed her head, and looked at Carl. "What is it that you want from me? I've done all I can to please you, and I can't do it anymore."

"I told you I got this. I'll have the money in the morning."

Carl then grabbed his cell phone and headed out the door, slamming it behind him. That night, Barbara cried like a baby, asking the Lord to see her through.

CHAPTER 11

Later that night, Carl Jr. looked out his window hoping his father would come home with the rent money so they wouldn't have to leave. Even though Carl Jr. thought it might be for the best, Mike and Shakira would've thought differently. It wasn't long before Carl was walking up the stairs.

"Honey, I'm home!" he yelled as he walked in the door, smiling gracefully while waving the money back and forth in front of his face. "Barbara, did you hear me? I've got the rent money."

When Barbara never answered, Carl finally got the hint and went to sleep on the couch, where he slept for the next few days. Things eventually blew over, and Carl was back in the room again. However, like always, it wasn't long before he started acting out again.

It was a Tuesday afternoon, and Reggie had come over to play. For some strange reason, Carl still wasn't over the beating Reggie had given him. For that reason, he told Carl Jr. to have his friend stay outside so he could rest. That didn't bother Carl Jr. none because he didn't want to be in the house anyway.

Carl Jr. told Reggie to give him a minute to get ready, and then they would head to Carl Jr.'s favorite hiding spot. It was a place he went when he just wanted to get away from the world and the mean people in it, his father being one of them.

On their way to the favorite spot, Reggie said, "Carl Jr., can I ask you something?"

"Yeah, Reggie."

"Why is my mother always sick and acts like it hurts for her just to walk to the kitchen?"

"I don't know, Reggie. Did you ask her?"

"Yes, and she always tells me that she's fine but just a little bit tired."

"Sounds like my mom," Carl Jr. said. "They're not going to tell us what's really going on because they don't want us to worry."

"Yeah, I guess that's what it is," said Reggie. "Mother is always telling us not to worry."

Carl Jr. knew something was really wrong, but he didn't want to tell Reggie. He didn't know how Reggie would react finding out that his mom had cancer and that she didn't have long to live. At least that's what Carl Jr. had overheard his mother telling one of her girlfriends on the phone one day.

Carl Jr. quickly changed the subject and began telling Reggie about some things he was planning to do when he got older. Time flew, and before they knew it, it was time to head back home. As they made their way back, Reggie expressed to his friend how much he meant to him.

"Carl Jr., I wish you were my brother and that we could stay together forever and ever."

"We are brothers, just from another mother. We will always be together."

Reggie smiled and told Carl Jr. that he would see him later.

As Carl Jr. made his way upstairs, he was anxious to tell his mother what Reggie said about his mother and how she wasn't doing too well. When he opened the door, Carl was sitting at the kitchen table having a conversation with Barbara about the same thing. Carl Jr. was confused as to how his father knew she was sick if Reggie didn't tell him.

Then again, he could have talked to Taisa, Carl Jr. thought.

Barbara quickly called Ann and asked her if everything was okay. Ann immediately started crying and sharing what the doctor had told her. Basically, she had to make a choice: have the baby and die, or get rid of the baby and live a little while longer.

"If I choose to have the baby, I don't know what I'm going to do."

Barbara got silent for a second, and tears began to roll down her face. "Oh God, Lord Jesus, my savior, touch my friend. Heal her from all her sicknesses. For you are the doctor, provider, and savior. Heal her, Lord; heal her."

Barbara continued praying for about ten minutes before she hung up with Ann. Then she went to her room and continued crying, while Carl sat there looking like he wanted to cry, too. Michael and Shakira had no clue as to what was going on. They just knew it wasn't the time for asking questions.

It was a strange week that week. It was like someone had already died. Even Old Man Johnson could see that something was wrong. One day, as Carl Jr. was on his way to the bus stop, Old Man Johnson asked him why everyone was looking so sad.

"Ms. Ann has cancer, and she doesn't have much longer to live."

"My prayers go out to her and her family, and I pray she gets better," he replied. "Are you okay?"

"Yes, but I'm worried about Reggie because he doesn't know. He thinks she's going to be okay."

"Don't worry. Everything's going to be okay. Carry on to school, Carl Jr."

No one said much about it after that week. It seemed as though no one wanted to deal with the fact that it was happening.

Sunday morning came, and Barbara told her children to get ready for church. Like always, Carl was sound asleep from being out all night getting drunk. He didn't even hear them leave. Barbara called Joe to pick them up and take them to church, forgetting that Carl had told her to never ride with him again. Carl Jr. knew she had forgotten, but he didn't say anything because he liked Joe and secretly wished he were their father.

"Good morning, kids," said Joe.

"Good morning," the children replied in unison.

"My, my, Mrs. Henley, don't you look extra lovely today. What's the special occasion?"

"Oh, stop. This dress is so old I just decided to put it on. It's been hanging up in my closet for almost two years."

"How come you don't wear it as much?"

"Long story," said Barbara.

"I'm listening."

"Well, since you insist on me telling you. Carl bought me this dress after he claimed I gained all this weight and couldn't fit any of my other dresses. He told me to try it on, and when I did, he got mad and told me that he had wasted his hard-earned money. He said I looked like Porky Pig in a high school prom dress. So, that made it hard for me to wear it."

"Well, if I may, I would like to correct that. It looks gorgeous on you, weight and all."

"Stop it, Joe. You're just trying to make me feel good."

"No, I'm serious, and that's coming straight from the heart. That dress looks good on you, and no one could wear it better."

Barbara looked out the cab window blushing all over. To Carl Jr., it was surreal seeing his mother feeling good about herself for a change.

That day, church service didn't last long because the choir had to go on a road trip, but like always, Joe was on time.

"How was church?" Joe asked.

"Pretty good," Barbara replied, "but how did you know church was letting out early?"

"I didn't. I just love waiting on you."

Barbara didn't comment because she realized Joe was hitting on her, and she didn't want to disrespect her husband.

"Ice cream, anybody?"

"Yeah! Yeah!" the children yelled out.

"Not this time," said Barbara, "but thanks anyway."

"Why not?" Shakira asked.

"Because I said so," her mother responded in an angry tone.

Feeling like he made Barbara feel slightly uncomfortable, Joe backed off and began singing.

"It's been too hard living, but I'm afraid to die. Just like a river, I've been running along the side. It's been a long, long time coming, but I know a change gonna come."

Barbara smiled. "That's that old Sam Cook. I used to love that song to death. I still do. That's what keeps me going, because I know a change is gonna come."

Before long, Barbara was singing, too. It was like she was feeling the same way. They sung that song all the way until Joe pulled the cab up in front of the apartments.

"Thanks for the ride, Joe."

"Anytime, Mrs. Henley, and I'm sorry I made you feel uncomfortable earlier."

"You're good. I just stress too much and need to start living a little."

"You said it, not me."

"Bye, Joe. See you next Sunday."

"Yes, ma'am. And I'll be here on time."

Barbara smiled while closing the door. Then she and the children made their way upstairs, not expecting to see Carl sitting on the couch with a mean look on his face.

"Hey, Carl," greeted Barbara.

"Hey my ass. I saw you grinnin' up in that cab driver's face. I thought I told you not to ride with him no more."

"Oh, Carl, please. What's the big deal? He's just taking us to church and back."

"You don't get it, do you? I don't care where you're going. I don't want him taking you nowhere! And that's my last time telling you. Next time, I'm going to beat somebody's ass."

"Why does it matter anyway? You don't want me. You never tell me I look good or smell good. All I hear from you is that I'm fat, you don't want to be here, and the kids are breaking you. Those are your favorite lines. And for the first time in a long time, Joe made me feel good about myself. He told me how beautiful I looked in the dress you bought for me and that it doesn't matter how much weight I've gained."

Why did she say that? Carl went off.

"What did you just say?"

Before she could get one word out, he ripped the dress off her and slapped her as hard as he could.

"Don't you ever in your fucking life tell me about what some other man told you. Are you crazy?"

Barbara didn't say a word. She just stood there and took the beating like it didn't even hurt her anymore.

"Get your damn hands off my mother! I'm tired of this shit!"

It was like the devil himself had walked in. Everything stopped. It was Michael yelling from across the room with a broom in his hand.

"What did you say, boy? I know you didn't curse at me. After all I do for your begging ass, you're gonna come at me like that? I'll beat your ass until you can't sit down."

When Carl went to grab Michael, Barbara grabbed his arm, screaming, "No, Carl! No! Carl, get off him, dammit!"

Carl turned around with a closed fist and punched her dead in her face, knocking her down to the floor. That's when Michael hit him with the broom in the back of the head. Carl turned around, grabbed Michael again, and started beating him like he was a grown man.

Once again, Carl Jr. just stood there speechless until he finally snapped out of it and ran downstairs to get Old Man Johnson, but to his surprise, he wasn't there.

What am I going to do now? he thought. Carl Jr. was scared to death. He ran back upstairs to see his mother getting up off the floor. Blood dripped everywhere as she continued trying to pull Carl off of Michael.

Inside, Carl Jr. was going crazy. Michael was getting beaten, his mother was bleeding like a running faucet, and Shakira was screaming at the top of her lungs.

"Stop it! Stop it!" Carl Jr. yelled, jumping in between them. "Do you remember what Mr. Johnson told you that night? Don't let that be you."

Carl stopped immediately. "What did you say, gay boy? You ain't no son of mine. Your little sister got more heart than you do. Every time something goes down, you runnin' like a little bitch. You think I'm scared of Old Man Johnson. You tell him when you see him that I just whipped your ass, your mother's ass, and your brother's ass."

He grabbed Carl Jr. and started slapping him around like a rag doll for about two minutes. Then, as he headed out the door, he turned back and said, "And this shit better be cleaned up when I get back."

As bad as he beat him, Carl Jr. never cried. He just wanted him to get off his mother and brother. He wanted to make sure everything was all right. Michael was the same way. The only thing the two boys were concerned about was their mother.

When Barbara couldn't stop her bleeding, she knew that she had to get to the hospital. The only person Carl Jr. could think of to call was Joe. So, he grabbed his mother's cell phone, located his number in the phone's address book, and called him.

"Hello, Mrs. Henley."

"No, Joe, this is Carl Jr. Mother needs a ride to the hospital!"

"What happened?"

"Carl punched her in the face."

"Don't move. I'm on the way."

Joe must have been right around the corner, because he got there in less than five minutes. When Joe got there, Barbara was still kind of out of it, so he had to carry her down the stairs.

"Why?" Joe asked.

"Because of you!" Michael burst out. Because of you, Joe. She told him that you made her feel like somebody, and he went off."

Joe got quiet for a moment as tears rolled down his face.

"I'm sorry, kids. I'm so sorry. I never meant for things to happen this way, not in a million years."

"Well, it did," said Michael.

"Calm down, Michael," Barbara said in a weak tone. "It's not Joe's fault; it's Carl's fault. He has a problem, a serious problem."

"It is my fault," interrupted Joe. "If I hadn't opened my big mouth, none of this would've ever happened."

They finally got to the hospital where the doctor examined Barbara and determined that her nose had been broken.

"What happened?" Dr. McIver asked.

"Oh, nothing. I fell on my way up the steps."

"Are you sure?"

"Yes, sir."

"If someone did this to you, Mrs. Henley, I'll have them locked up."

"Oh no. No one did this. I truly fell."

Barbara never changed her story, and the children knew not to say anything. Joe waited outside for about three hours before they came out.

"You okay, Mrs. Henley?"

"Yes. I'm just a little tired. Thanks for waiting on us."

"Anytime," he replied.

That ride was the quietest ride they ever had with Joe. Carl Jr. could see the anger in Joe's face. It was the same look Old Man Johnson had a while back.

When they pulled up at the apartment, Joe got out to help Barbara up the stairs.

"I got it from here, Joe, but thanks anyway."

With tears rolling down his face, Joe got back in the cab, then looked at Carl Jr. and said, "Make sure you take care of your mother for me. Once again, I'm sorry." Then he drove off slowly, while wiping the tears from his face.

As they approached the apartment building, there was Old Man Johnson sitting on the porch looking worried.

"Where have y'all been? I've been looking all over for y'all, and no one knew where y'all were at."

Before anyone could say anything, Old Man Johnson asked Barbara, "What happened to your face?"

"I fell on the steps."

"That's a lie. Carl did that, didn't he?"

"No, Mr. Johnson."

"Don't lie to me, Barbara."

"I'm not, Mr. Johnson."

Carl Jr. couldn't take it anymore. He had to tell Old Man Johnson what had happened.

"It was Carl. He beat me, Michael, and Mother like rag dolls. Then he left us there bleeding and crying."

"Go home and lock the door," Old Man Johnson told her. "He's gone too far this time. I promised you and those kids that I would be here for y'all, and I wasn't. Damn you, Carl."

"It's okay," Barbara said. "The Lord's gonna work it out."

"Let's hope he do before I do," Old Man Johnson responded as he walked into his apartment and slammed the door behind him.

Carl Jr. was suddenly scared and wondered what he had done, because he remembered what Old Man Johnson told Carl he would do if Carl hurt them.

"Come on, kids, it's late. Gotta get some sleep. It's been a long day."

That night went by slow. Every minute on the hour, Carl Jr. looked at the clock panting, wondering if Carl would show up. Hour after hour, still no Carl and no sign of Old Man Johnson. Carl Jr. just knew in his heart that Carl was dead.

He finally dozed off, but was quickly awakened by the key being inserted into the door lock. *Am I dreaming or is Carl really coming in?* Minutes later, he heard Carl in the kitchen mumbling.

"Damn, I'm hungry and ain't shit in here to cook."

Carl lay on the couch in his usual spot the way he always did after he had too much to drink.

Carl Jr. was confused. *Why didn't Mr. Johnson do something to him? Was he faking about being a stone cold killer or did he not find Dad in time?* Having exhausted all the options, Carl Jr. finally fell asleep.

The next morning, he woke up to see his father still lying on the couch.

Barbara woke him, saying, "Either you leave or we leave, because I can't do this anymore."

"You're right," said Carl. "As soon as I find me a place, I'm gonna get the hell out of here. I'm tired of being broke and unhappy."

"The sooner the better, Carl. My kids don't deserve this, having to watch their father physically and mentally abuse their mother. This has been going on too long."

"Damn right. I should have left a long time ago when you gained all that weight and stopped looking like somebody."

"You might be right. Maybe the Lord don't like me and don't hear my cry, but I know one day a change is gonna come."

"Face it, Barbara. You ain't gonna be no more than what you are now. Didn't you say it was already written on how your life is going to be? Your God knew it before it happened. So, why would you have faith in someone that would let you go through what you have been going through all these years?"

"The Bible says you got to go through before you come out," Barbara replied. "I have to believe that. That little beating you call yourself putting on me is nothing compared to the beating Jesus took when he was nailed to the cross. He died for your sins, still kept the faith, and asked God to forgive us because we know not what we do."

"Whatever, Barbara. Say what you want. If God was coming, he would have been here by now."

"The devil is a liar, Carl. He might not come when you want him, but he'll be here right on time. I'm going to wait as long as I have to 'cause I know in my heart that a change is truly gonna come."

"Well, you wait on. I'm gettin' the hell out of here as soon as I find something."

From that day, Carl Jr. counted down the days until his father found something.

CHAPTER 12

A month had gone by, and Carl still hadn't found anything. He began hanging out more and more every night. There was one particular night when Carl came home and his cell phone wouldn't stop ringing. When he answered, someone on the other end could be heard yelling, "I want my motherfucking money! I want my money!"

Right then and there, Carl Jr. knew his father had gotten himself into something he was unable to get out of because he had that scared look on his face. The very next day, Barbara got a call from Taisa.

"Carl owes my boyfriend a whole lot of money."

"For what?" Barbara asked.

Taisa hesitated for a second. "I really hate to say this, Mrs. Henley, but Carl has been doing drugs for a minute now. That's why he's always at Joe's Poker House. That's where he gets high at."

Barbara was shocked and speechless. "How much does he owe?" she finally asked.

"Twenty-two hundred dollars."

"Twenty who? How did he get to owe someone so much money?"

"It was me, Mrs. Henley. I made Brian credit him here and there for a long time. And now that we're not talking anymore, Brian wants his money. That's just another way to get me back."

"I don't know what to tell you to do. I don't have that kind of money."

"You don't know Brian, Mrs. Henley. He's not taking no for an answer."

"What's that got to do with us?"

"If Brian can't get Carl, he'll go after the family."

Barbara dropped the phone. "Kids, get your things 'cause we have to leave."

"Where are we going?" Shakira inquired.

"I don't know, but we have to leave here."

"Why?" asked Michael.

"Don't worry about why. Just do as I say."

After grabbing whatever belongings they could carry, they headed down the stairs, where they ran into Old Man Johnson.

"Going somewhere?" he asked.

"Yeah, but don't know where," Barbara responded.

"Why is that?"

"Carl done got himself into something he can't get out of, and now they're coming after us."

"Who are they?"

"Brian, the drug dealer."

"You talking about Taisa's boyfriend?"

"Yes. Carl owes him a lot of money, and I don't have it to give him."

"Damn you, Carl," Old Man Johnson said as he kicked the chair off the porch.

"Don't worry. Joe's going to come pick us up and take us to his house for a while."

"Okay, but y'all be safe out there."

"We will. Just watch the house until we get back."

"I sure will, Barbara."

Two days went by. No Carl, no nothing. Barbara's cell phone went off, and it was Taisa again. This time, she was crying her eyes out.

"What's wrong, Taisa? Is Ann okay?"

"Yes, mother's fine. It's Brian. He's dead! Someone killed him and his partners last night, and no one knows who did it."

Barbara was both happy and sad. She was sad at Taisa's loss, but happy that her and her children could go home and not have to worry about someone coming after them.

Carl must have heard the news himself, because he showed up at the house at the same time they did.

"How could you, Carl? How could you leave us in harm's way while you hide out because you owe someone a bunch of money?"

"Didn't you say your God would protect you as long as you kept the faith?"

"He will."

"Then why in the hell do you need me?"

"What kind of man are you to not give a damn about his own family? Lord, forgive me. The devil is a liar."

"The kind of man that puts food on this table."

"Not this table."

"Whatever, woman."

Carl Jr. could see in his mother's eyes that she was tired. Not scared anymore, he stood up.

"Carl, all you've done is down my mother, making her feel like a nobody. You're the one that's a nobody. My mother is a strong righteous woman that has a sorry man trying to drag her down."

Carl pointed his finger at him. "You better watch your mouth."

"Or what? You're gonna beat me again?"

"You damn right."

When Carl started approaching him, he took off out the door to his favorite spot in the woods until he calmed down. A few hours went by before he made his way back home.

As soon as Carl Jr. opened the door, his mother grabbed him and asked, "Are you okay?"

"Yes, I'm fine."

"I was worried because Carl took off looking for you."

After that day, no one heard from Carl again.

CHAPTER 13

A few months went by and still no Carl. Things slowly began to change. Old Man Johnson was back to reading his daily paper. Joe was there every Sunday morning to take them to church and ease his way into Barbara's heart. It was like a dream come true.

The funny part about it was no one asked about Carl. It was like everyone was scared to talk about him, because if they did, he might turn back up. A few more months went by and everything was lovely, except for Barbara kind of missing Carl.

Carl had been gone for close to six months, when Barbara got a call from Ann. She was about to have her baby and wanted everyone she called "family" to be there. It was sad because Reggie and Taisa had no clue their mother was only going to live approximately a few weeks after she had the baby. That day, Barbara and her children loaded up in Joe's cab and headed to the hospital to see Ann before she went into the delivery room.

When they got there, Ann broke the bad news to her children, and that night, Reggie cried and cried until he cried himself to sleep. Taisa didn't take the news bad. Carl had already told her that her mother had breast cancer and didn't have long to live. That was why Taisa decided to leave Brian alone and go back home.

Shockingly, sharing the news that she didn't have long to live wasn't the only reason Ann called everyone to the hospital. She had something else to say that knocked everyone off their feet. Even Joe was shocked.

"I've been hiding something for many years because I didn't know how to come out and say it. But, I know I'm on my deathbed, and I've got to get right with God. Barbara, I've wanted to tell you so many times, but it wouldn't come out. That's why I would always break down and cry when we talked.

"Barbara, I would understand if you never forgive me 'cause what I've done should never be forgiven. But, thanks to God, our forgiving God, he sees no sin greater than the other."

Ann started crying and could barely get her words out. "The baby I'm having is Carl's, and Taisa and Reggie are his children, as well."

This time, not only was Carl Jr. speechless, but everyone in the room was silent, while Barbara just stood there looking in one direction.

"How could you, Ann? How could you cross me like that?"

"Barbara, I'm sorry. It was way before you came along. Carl and me had an understanding when I had Taisa. We would keep things a secret because I wasn't ready to settle down. So, we went on for years keeping it to ourselves. That's when he met you and fell in love all over again. That's also when I realized I wanted to settle down, but it was too late. He was in love with you, and I hated that with a passion. So, I tried to get back at him by having Reggie. That's when everything went downhill.

"Carl was upset and scared that if you found out, he would lose his family that he loved so dearly. That's when he started drinking, trying to squabble the pain. I watched Carl cry for many nights, screaming how he was sorry for putting you through so much pain. He said if he could turn back the hands of time, he would do it all over again the right way. That's when I realized how much he really loved his family, and I didn't want to break that up.

"Barbara, I'm sorry I had to come to this point in my life for me to have to tell you this way, but I need you to care for my kids when I'm gone. They have nobody and nowhere to go. I beg you, Barbara, here on my deathbed…promise me that you will take care of my kids."

Barbara never said a word. She just stood there looking off into a lost world. The look on her face was as cold as a winter night.

"Barbara, I'm sorry. Please forgive me."

"Joe, let's go," Barbara finally said. "Get me out of here. I've heard all I can bear."

"Please, Barbara. Please!"

While staring Ann dead in her eyes, Barbara prayed, "God, forgive her and have mercy on her soul, for she know not what she has done. She will have to answer for her deceit." She then looked at her three children and said, "Let's go."

On her way out the door, Barbara stopped to tell Ann, "You better be glad there is a God and that he's a forgiving one. If there wasn't, you would surely burn in hell."

"Barbara, come back!" Ann yelled as Barbara and her children walked out the door.

No one said anything the whole way home, not even Joe. That night, Barbara sat there just staring off into a world of her own.

Two days later, she got a call from the hospital telling her that Ann had died. She left Barbara custody of the kids, the beneficiary of her insurance policy, and a will made out only in her name.

After hanging up the phone, Barbara screamed to the top of her lungs, "Why me? Why me, Lord? What did I do to deserve so much pain? I serve you. I love you more than I love myself, but the rain keeps falling on my face. What is it, Lord, that you want me to do?"

Barbara sat there crying her heart out. Then, all of a sudden, she stopped and a smile came across her face. It was like a ton of weight was lifted off her shoulders and a new woman was born.

"Carl Jr., call Joe. I got some kids to pick up."

Doing as he was told, Carl Jr. grabbed the phone to place the call. However, he was both understanding and confused at the same time. *Could this be happening? Mother's taking in our half-brother and half-sister. Where are they going to sleep, and how is Mother going to feed them? Will Michael be able to deal with Reggie? Is Taisa going to respect Mother?*

Carl Jr. asked himself about a hundred questions, trying to get himself to understand what was happening. Minutes later, Joe was out front honking the horn.

"Let's go before this old woman changes her mind."

As they rushed down the stairs, ready to tell Joe the good news, they ran into Old Man Johnson.

"What's the rush?" he asked.

Before anyone else could answer, Shakira burst out, "We're going to pick up our new brother and sister."

"Oh yeah?"

"Long story," said Barbara. "I'll have to fill you in when we get back."

"You do that," Old Man Johnson replied. "I'll be sitting right here waiting on y'all to get back."

They then jumped in the cab, and before Joe took off, Shakira started telling him the story.

"For real?" said Joe.

"Yes," Barbara responded.

"What made you decide to do that?"

"I spoke to God, and this is his wish."

Joe smiled. "I'm proud of you. I've been praying for this day ever since we left the hospital."

"Why were you so concerned?" she asked.

"Because I know how it is to not have a family and to feel like nobody wants you. I know what it would mean to those kids to have someone as special as you to raise them and love them like you love your own."

"I don't know, Joe. Raising five kids and a newborn won't be easy."

"Don't worry, Mrs. Henley. I'm going to be here with you every step of the way. We're going to raise these kids together."

78

Barbara looked at Joe and smiled. "All I ask is for God to lead the way."

"I think He's been doing that the whole time."

It was unbelievable. It was happening right before Carl Jr.'s very eyes. Things were changing, and they were finally getting the family he had dreamt about for many years.

"We're here," Joe announced.

"Let me go in by myself," Barbara told him.

"No problem. We'll be right here when you get back."

When Barbara went into the hospital, she saw Reggie and Taisa standing outside the room crying. They didn't know what was going to happen to them and their newborn sister.

"It's okay. I'm here now. Y'all are coming with me."

"For real?" Reggie asked. "Taisa told me no one wanted us and that we would have to split up."

"That's not true. I want y'all and so do the kids."

"You mean me and Carl Jr. are going to be living together?"

"Yes, Reggie."

Reggie grabbed Barbara, hugged her as tight as he could, and said, "Promise you'll never leave us."

"I won't, baby. As long as I live, I will be right here for you and all my family."

Barbara then hugged Taisa. "I'm going to need you to help with the newborn."

"Don't worry, Mrs. Henley. I won't let you down."

"So where's that little baby girl y'all have been talking about?"

"Down the hall, on the right. The first one in front of the window."

It was about two and a half hours before they all came out to the cab.

"I can't take the baby from the hospital without a car seat. Besides, we don't have enough room for all of us. So, if you could take the kids home and come back to get me and the baby, I would greatly appreciate it."

"Yes, ma'am," Joe replied. "I will be back in a jiffy."

"And don't forget the car seat."

"Don't worry, I won't."

While waiting for Joe to return, Barbara sat there staring at the baby and smiling. "You look just like your old daddy."

That night, everyone stayed up until three in the morning laughing and playing with the baby until she finally went to sleep.

Carl Jr. didn't go to sleep, though. It was like waiting on Christmas. He was happy all over again. Before he knew it, it was six o'clock in the morning, and the baby was up crying, wanting something to eat.

"I got it," said Taisa. "Go back to sleep. I know it's been a long day for you, Mrs. Henley."

"Are you sure?"

"Yes, ma'am. I've had plenty of practice raising Reggie."

Barbara crawled back into bed.

Everything was perfect, and all was going better than expected. Everyone was getting along. Taisa was helping Barbara around the house. Joe came by on the regular. And Old Man Johnson helped Barbara with the food and bills until the insurance money came in.

CHAPTER 14

Four years went by and everything was perfect. Joe and Barbara had been seeing each other on a regular basis, but nothing too serious happened between them because she hadn't gotten her divorce. Carl was still nowhere to be found. The money from Ann's insurance finally came, which meant Barbara no longer had to stress about paying the bills and feeding the children.

Old Man Johnson acted like their long lost grandfather who was making up for lost time. Anything the children wanted he gave to them. Michael was still on the path to becoming teacher. Shakira was an 'A' student and belonged to every school activity. She always tried to outdo Michael. Reggie was doing well, also. It was his last year of high school, and he got a full ride to the University of South Carolina on a football scholarship. Taisa was in her last year at Winthrop University, and it was Carl Jr.'s third year at the Medical University of South Carolina. He was at the top of his class in the biophysics program, working on a chemical solution to make some of the world's finest jewelry.

It was like a dream come true. Everything was perfect, until one afternoon around four o'clock on graduation day at Winthrop University. They were at the pre-graduation concert hosted by Winthrop's True Vine Gospel Choir.

Carl Jr., Michael, Shakira, Reggie, Barbara, Joe, Old Man Johnson, and little Faith all went down to see Taisa receive her bachelor's degree. She was also made an officer in the United States Army for serving four years in the ROTC program. That day was one of the proudest days of the Henley family's lives.

Barbara was in tears. Not tears of pain, but tears of joy to see her adopted daughter do so well after all she had been through. It was truly a blessing, and she was a role model for the rest of the children. It was like God had finally answered their prayers. There was Taisa, serving the Lord, doing the right thing, and about to go into the world to make a difference.

All of a sudden, the sweet dream took an unexpected turn. Taisa somehow became dizzy as she sung her heart out on stage, and then she passed out.

"What happened?" Reggie asked.

"Oh, sis can't handle all this excitement, so she goes and passes out. Wait 'til she comes to. I'm gonna clown her like no other," said Michael.

Barbara got up and went backstage to make sure Taisa was okay, while the rest of them sat there and watched the remainder of the show. No one paid any mind until Joe spoke out.

"Where's Barbara? Why is she taking so long? Taisa only passed out…"

Before he could finish the rest of his sentence, Barbara came around the corner with a grim look on her face.

"What's wrong, Barbara?" Joe asked.

"I really don't know, but they said she had to be rushed to the emergency room."

Everything got quiet.

"What now? Graduation is in an hour, and we'll never make it back in time."

"Let's hope we do," said Reggie. "She's been waiting on this day for a long time."

"I know," Barbara replied, "but I guess now we'll just head to the hospital."

The whole way there no one said a thing. As they pulled up to the hospital, Reggie finally spoke.

"I'll stay in the car until y'all come back. The last time I was at the hospital it wasn't good."

"Don't think like that," Barbara told him. "Always hope for the best."

"I'm going because I've got some clowning to do," said Michael.

"I'll wait here, because I don't like hospitals either," Old Man Johnson voiced.

"Okay," Barbara responded. "We'll be back in a few."

It seemed like the closer they got, the further away the hospital seemed to get. When they finally got there, the doctor came out from the back area of the emergency room and pulled mother to the side. Right then and there, Carl Jr. had a feeling that something wasn't right.

"Can we see her?" asked Shakira.

"Not now," replied the nurse, who was standing by the door to make sure no one came in or out.

"What's going on?" asked Joe. "This doesn't make any sense, all this for a little dehydration? Something else must be going on."

The nurse responded, "You have to talk to the doctor about that."

"And who might you be?"

"I'm just the doctor's assistant."

"And you mean to tell me that you don't know what's going on?"

"I do, but you'll have to speak to the doctor on that matter. I'm not authorized to give any information about the patient."

"Whatever, lady," Joe said, blowing her off.

That's when Carl Jr. got up and pulled Joe to the side because he could see that Joe was getting very angry. Barbara walked over to join them.

"Things are not looking too good. Someone needs to go get Reggie because Taisa is asking to see him."

As Carl Jr. took off downstairs, he thought about what he would tell Reggie since he didn't even know exactly what was going on because Barbara never shared that information with him. When he got to the car, he saw Old Man Johnson and Reggie laughing and playing, not knowing it was all about to end.

"What's keeping y'all so long? She hasn't woken up yet?" Reggie asked.

Carl Jr. paused for a second and dropped his head, letting him know something was wrong.

"What's wrong, Carl Jr.? Tell me Taisa's okay."

He never lifted his head.

"Carl Jr., do you hear me? What's going on with Taisa?"

"Not good, Reggie. Mother said Taisa wanted to see you before talking to anyone else."

"What's wrong?"

"I don't know. Mother never told me. I was just asked to tell you to come up, and that was it."

Reggie grabbed his friend's hand and said, "Hold my hand as we walk up the stairs."

Reggie's hand shook all the way there, and sweat dripped from his palms. When they reached the outside of Taisa's room, Barbara told Reggie to go in. As Reggie went in, he looked back at them with fear on his face, not knowing what to expect as he closed the door behind him.

It was the longest thirty minutes of their lives, sitting there waiting to hear what was going on. Reggie came out, but not like he went in. Carl Jr. could see the anger written all over him.

"Is she okay?" Barbara asked.

"Hell no, she's not okay."

"Watch your mouth," she said in a stern voice. "I still want my respect."

"Yes, ma'am. It's just I don't understand. You told me that my God was a good God and that he would take care of us as long as we kept the faith."

"That's true, Reggie. God knows everything, and he knows what's best for us."

"How can you say that, Mrs. Henley, after all we've been through and are still going through? When will it stop? Does He not hear our cry? Does He not know we're tired? Lord knows ever since my mother died, I've been on my knees every night praying that he watch over all my family and me. And this is the best He can do?"

"Watch what you say, Reggie."

"No, Mrs. Henley. We've been doing right by God for a long time, and the only one that's getting the victory is Satan. What do we have to do to get His attention? Sacrifice all of us? No more, Mrs. Henley. I'm sorry. I love you to death, but your God ain't no good God, and he doesn't answer no prayers."

"Reggie, know what you're saying."

"I know what I'm saying. My sister has been serving him like no other. Reading and studying the Bible day in and day out; telling the world how good He is, how He will make a way, and how He can work miracles. And this is how he repays her? By taking her life after all she's done for Him? What God does that? All these bad people out here in this world doing all the wrong things, yet he still takes her first. Someone who can make a difference. Someone that's a role model."

"Reggie, God works in mysterious ways, and you should never question him on his decisions."

"Well, maybe you shouldn't question. Right now, as far as I'm concerned, there ain't no God."

"Reggie, please, I'm begging you, for you know not what you are saying."

"Like I said, until He's able to heal my sister, I know there ain't no God."

"No, Reggie. No, Reggie, don't do this."

"Don't worry about me. I'll make it on my own, and I'll see y'all when I see y'all."

"Reggie, come back!"

"Let him go, Mother. He's just upset right now," Carl Jr. told her.

That day, Taisa talked to each of them and told them not to worry because she was going home. She said, "I can't wait, because I know that it's a better place."

Day in and day out, they all took turns sitting and talking to Taisa as she grew weaker. Not one day went by where she didn't ask about Reggie, but he was nowhere to be found. Carl Jr. became worried because he knew what Reggie was capable of doing. But, he had no clue as to where he could be. Barbara grew worried because Taisa was getting sicker by the minute and really wanted to see Reggie. It seemed like that was the only reason she was clinging to life.

"Go find him," said Barbara. "Go find him fast, because the doctor said it won't be long before Taisa passes away."

Carl Jr. was starting to feel like Reggie. All they had been through and never once had they lost their faith, yet God never seemed to come through. Even though he knew his mother would never lie to them about God and what he can do, it was like for some strange reason, He just didn't want to do it for Carl Jr.'s family. It was like someone or something had placed a curse on their whole family and everything around them. And it didn't seem like it would be letting up no time soon. He never got too intense with that conversation about God's reasons for doing what he does because Carl Jr. knew better than to do so. Therefore, at the end of the day, he just carried on.

"Go find him!" Barbara demanded in an angry tone.

Quickly, Carl Jr. stood up and started making his way to the door, but Old Man Johnson stopped him.

"I got it, Carl Jr. I have an idea of where Reggie might be from the conversation we had a few days ago."

Since Carl Jr. didn't have a clue where to start looking, he didn't hesitate to sit back down.

"I'll come with you," Joe offered.

"No, stay here with the family and make sure everything is okay."

"I will," said Joe. "I will."

As the hours passed by, everyone sat there staring into space. They counted down the time Taisa had left on earth. It was devastating to see her get so weak and old in just a few weeks. They watched her change right before their eyes, and it was something Carl Jr. wished to never experience again in his life.

Another day went by, but still no Reggie. Taisa was on her last leg. Her vision was going, and her memory was going even faster. Carl Jr. had witnessed all that he could handle. He couldn't stand seeing her like that anymore. So, that day, he made his mind up that it would be his last visit. Though everyone else still held on and prayed that God would step in and Taisa would be healed, Carl Jr. didn't feel that way because he felt like Taisa didn't want to come back. To him, it seemed like she was sacrificing herself for them.

"Mother, Mother! Reggie's back! Reggie's back!" Shakira yelled.

When Carl Jr. looked around, he saw his best friend standing there he looking lost as ever.

"Thank God," said Barbara. "He heard my prayers."

Reggie didn't say a word. He just walked into the room where Taisa was, but not twenty minutes later, Reggie was on his way out of the room.

"She's gone," Reggie told them. "She's gone, and she told me to tell y'all not to worry because she's gone home to be with her holy family."

Everything stopped. Barbara grabbed her mouth and leaned her head against the wall as she screamed. Carl Jr. stared at Reggie and watched him burst into tears.

As Reggie shook like he was going into a mild seizure, Carl Jr. ran over, hugged him tighter than ever, and told him, "Everything will be alright."

"No, Carl Jr.! No! Taisa's dead. It's not going to be alright. She's gone, and she's never coming back."

"It's okay, Reggie. She's gone to a better place."

"There ain't no damn better place. We need her here to help raise us, and He took that from us. What God does that? Why not me, Carl Jr.? Why not me? I'd rather him take my life than hers. She was the perfect person. And me, I'm just a nobody hanging on by a thread."

"No, that's not true. You are somebody, and we love you. Taisa would say the same thing if she were here. We got to be strong. We got to do it for Taisa."

"Taisa's gone, Carl Jr. Get over it."

"Not true, Reggie. She lives in our hearts and will always be remembered."

"No more, Carl Jr.! No more of your God stories. No more believing in someone that's not real. I'm gonna get it how I live."

"Don't do this to yourself, Reggie. Do this for Taisa."

"I told you Taisa's gone. I promised her that I'd take care of my little sister, and that's what I'll do. See y'all when I see y'all. I got things to do."

That night, everyone cried continuously, trying hard to understand what happened.

Barbara cried out, throwing her hand towards the sky, "What is it, Lord, that I'm not doing right? What makes these cruel things happen to us? I pray, Lord, day in and day out. I fast for weeks at a time. I give you all the glory, and I've never questioned what you do. But, this time, I have to ask why, Lord? Why us? Why do we suffer so much when we have so little? I'm tired, Lord. I give up. I surrender. I put it all in your hands because there's nothing else I can do."

No one said a word after that. They didn't know where to go from there.

Days went by and nothing was the same. Everyone waited on that sad day to come and go. No one knew if Reggie would be there because no one had heard from him since that day at the hospital.

The day of the funeral finally came, and everyone prepared differently. The service was held on July 25th at 2:00 p.m. at Friendship Baptist Church in Conway, South Carolina. The person officiating was Reverend Dr. Lee Pete, one of Taisa's favorite preachers. Barbara made sure that everything she thought Taisa would like, she had.

Not only was the president of Winthrop College there to present her with her degree, the military was there also to give her medals for becoming an officer in the US Army. They had it laid out. Six soldiers toted the casket, and six soldiers carried guns and the American Flag to place over her casket. It was unbelievable. Taisa was being treated like the queen she had been in life.

Everyone looked their best, all of her friends from college, her old high school classmates, and her family and childhood friends. Everyone was there except Reggie. Service started on time, with everyone being greeted by the first song from the church choir. Reverend Pete then made his regards to the family and began preaching. He said how wonderful Taisa was and how he had watched her turn her life around to become the lady she was.

Not long after, Barbara got up to speak. "I was glad to have Taisa as a daughter. I loved her, and she's gone to a better place. One day we will meet again. Taisa really loved her brother. He meant so much to her. She would want him here to see how much we all love her. Know that God works in mysterious ways, and He didn't take Taisa for nothing. He took her because he knew she was ready."

Barbara started to cry as she continued talking. "I know many of you knew Taisa and how she felt about God. How she was always talking about Him. None of us know just how close she really was but God. When I went to clean out her dorm room, I found a box full of letters that Taisa had written to the Lord, telling Him how much she loved Him and that she was ready to come home any day now. I guess God answered her prayers and brought His daughter on home."

Before she could say another word, the church doors flew wide open and a voice yelled out, "Well, why didn't He answer my prayers? I prayed every day and night that He would bring my sister back, and He never answered. Now does that sound like an understanding God to you? Or does that sound like a selfish God? Y'all tell me."

"Young man, respect my church," said Reverend Pete, "or I'll have you removed."

"Come move me!" Reggie shouted.

"No, no. Let him talk," Barbara said. "That was his sister, and right now, he's mad with world."

"That's right, I'm mad, but not with the world. I'm mad with your God. He took the only thing in this world that loved me the way she did. Why me, Lord?" Reggie yelled out as he made his way to the front of the church.

He cried his eyes out while staring hard at Taisa's casket. Reggie looked tired like he hadn't had any sleep since the day he left the hospital. Everyone was speechless as they watched Reggie fall to his knees by the side of the casket, screaming, "Why, Lord! Why?"

Barbara went over and knelt down beside him. "Everything is going to be okay."

"No, Mrs. Henley. God took my Taisa from me!"

It was like a chain reaction. One person started crying, and then the next thing you know, the whole church was crying and hollering, holding the person next to them. Barbara finally got Reggie up and calmed him down. Then she walked him towards the bench where she was sitting.

"Mind if I speak?" Reggie asked. "I have a poem that I wrote for Taisa."

"Sure," Barbara replied, then walked him up to the podium.

"Can I have your undivided attention? Reggie has a poem that he wrote for his sister, and he wants to read it."

Still wiping tears from their eyes, everyone looked at Reggie and waited for him to begin. Reggie stood there for a minute before saying anything.

Then, all of a sudden, Reggie belted out, "Said that I'm ready. I'm ready to die. Said that I wonder if the Lord ever heard my cry. Thinking back on how it used to be. The sounds of my sister are all now history. Remember the times she would always say, 'I'll be glad when I die and leave this place'. But who would ever think it would happen like this 'cause never before was I granted a wish. I'm asking myself why couldn't it be me, but then I thought God don't like ugliness. And even though I know true facts are true facts, there's a yearning that she'll be back. And if not now, well, in the days to come. If not then, well, the life after that one. Until that day, it's all hope and mysteries, true facts and memories.

"Said that I'm ready. I'm ready to die. Said that I wonder if the Lord ever heard my cry. And now that she has passed that's a part of me gone. But like they say, life goes on. So who's to blame for this heartache and shame wrapped up in guilt which makes it pain. No more days when I will see her sleep. No more days when I will hear her speak. No more days of us fussing and fighting. No more days of us playing and bike riding. No more days of just her being here, but many more days that I will shed a tear. Not the tears of pain, but the tears of joy because I know she's in the heavens above. And in that place, I know she's safe. No more pain and no more heartache. But until that day, it's all hopes and mysteries, true facts and memories.

"Said that I'm ready. I'm ready to die. Said that I wonder if the Lord ever heard my cry. I remember the exact words that my sister told me. 'Just because I'm sick doesn't mean you can't hold me. Reggie, don't you worry 'cause soon I'm going home, and if I don't make it, I still want my room.' It took me 'til this day to realize what she meant. Her home wasn't home, because her home was heaven sent. Until this day, I fail to understand, but who am I to question the Almighty Man? So, until that day, it's all hopes and mysteries, true facts and memories.

"Said that I'm ready. I'm ready to die. Said that I wonder if the Lord ever heard my cry."

Reggie then looked up at the ceiling and yelled, "Why Lord," before making his way back to the casket.

Barbara got up and grabbed him. "She's gone now. We have to let her go."

"No!" said Reggie. "No more, Lord! No more!" he screamed to the top of his lungs.

"It's okay, Reggie. It's okay," Barbara said while trying to comfort him.

Seeing that Reggie was getting more and more upset, Carl Jr. stood up, walked to the front, grabbed Reggie, and hugged him as tight as he could.

"I love you. You're my brother, and I ain't going nowhere. I'll be here for you no matter what, like always."

Reggie laid his head on Carl Jr.'s shoulder crying his eyes out. "Promise me that you'll never leave me like Taisa."

"I promise."

"I'm scared, Carl Jr. Scared to be alone. I don't think I can make it."

"You are not alone. Me and the family love you just as much, and we will always be here."

Reggie finally calmed down and made his way out the door. Carl Jr. didn't stick around for the rest of the funeral because he knew Reggie couldn't handle it and he wanted to be there for him. So, he and Reggie went to their favorite spot in the woods to reminisce about the good old days, which weren't many. They stayed there until it was almost dark.

"Let's go home, Reggie, before they start worrying about us."

"You're right. I've put them through enough with me acting like a fool and blaming God for what happened to Taisa."

"We all go through our ups and downs, not understanding why things go the way they do. I've been fighting all my life trying to understand why our dad was the way he was when he had so many people loving him the way we do."

"I know, right? Who would have ever thought your dad was my dad, too. I guess that's why we're so close."

"Who knows? Maybe God has something good in store for us down the road. You know what they say: trouble don't last always."

"It's gonna work out, Carl Jr. I have a plan. One day, we are going to have more money than we can count."

"And may I ask how you plan to do that?"

"That's my little secret. You just continue doing what you're doing, and I'll do the rest."

"Say no more," Carl Jr. said. "The ball's in your hand. Speaking of ball, we're waiting on you to be the next Mike Vick."

"Yeah, right. The way things are going around here, I'll be happy to see the next five years," Reggie replied.

"Faith, bro. Faith. You've got to have that before anything can work."

"You're right. From here on out, I promise you that I'm gonna live on faith."

"And if you do that, I promise you that we'll be more than okay in the future," Carl Jr. told him.

"You have yourself a deal, brother," said Reggie, as they chuckled all the way home.

CHAPTER 15

"Where have you two been all this time?" Barbara asked. "We were worried to death."

"It's my fault, Mother. I had Reggie at my little spot in the woods telling him all my war stories."

"War stories my butt. Don't you guys ever do that to me again."

"Yes, Mother," said Reggie. "I promise we won't."

Everything got quiet as a tear rolled down Barbara's face. She was astounded and overwhelmed that Reggie had called her mother.

"Go to your room and don't come out until I tell y'all to."

"Yes, ma'am," the two boys replied simultaneously as they made their way to the room.

"Carl Jr., you know what, man? I think I'm going to love my new family as much as I did my old family."

"Me, too, Reggie. This one feels like the right one."

That night, Carl Jr. and Reggie talked for hours about what they were going to do when they got older. Reggie expressed that he wanted to be the football star that everyone dreamed about. He said he was going to take care of the whole family, including Old Man Johnson and Joe, the cab driver.

Carl Jr.'s dream wasn't too far from that. He wanted to become an expert chemist and create a chemical that he could use to make one-of-a-kind jewelry. Then he wanted to sell it for millions of dollars so he could buy all of his family members big houses and nice cars. He wanted to make sure no one would have to want for anything ever again.

It wasn't long after that before Barbara came to the door. "Carl Jr. and Reggie, y'all can come out now. Dinner's ready."

"Yes, ma'am."

"And make sure y'all wash y'all hands."

"We will, Mother."

Carl Jr. washed up first and entered the dining area to see all of his family members seated around one big table. Old Man Johnson and Joe were on the couch.

"What's taking Reggie so long?" Barbara asked her son.

"Reggie had a lot of washing to do. He hasn't washed in the last few weeks."

"I heard that, Carl Jr.," said Reggie as he entered the room.

Everyone busted out laughing.

"Okay. Gather around the table everyone so I can bless the food."

"Let me say the blessing," Reggie said.

"If you wish," Barbara replied.

After everyone had lowered their head, Reggie began with the prayer. "I stand here before this wonderful dinner, prepared by my wonderful mother, which will soon be eaten by my wonderful family. So, I ask you, Lord, to bless this food for which we are about to devour. And bless this family, for there will be many more to come. Amen."

"Not bad," said Michael. "Didn't know you had it in you."

"I'm working on it."

That night, they were one big happy family, and for the first time in his life, Carl Jr. saw his family and friends happy at one time. It was like God had finally heard their prayers.

*****

Everything was going as planned. Michael did well in school, like always. Shakira was growing up right before their eyes. Reggie was the man at USC. And Carl Jr. was doing his thing at MUSC.

Carl Jr. became a chemistry madman. There wasn't anything he couldn't whip up to perfection. He received many awards for his many achievements and was well on his way to finishing up his one-of-a-kind solution. He could feel it getting closer and closer to being perfected. Meaning he would soon be a rich man who made it so his family would never have to work again. It was destined to happen.

As for Barbara, she had her hands full with Faith. Since Taisa was gone, she was having the time of her life raising her. Barbara watched her learn to crawl and sit up, and she blushed every time she mumbled anything that sounded like the word Ma.

Joe was over every chance he got. He helped Barbara with whatever she needed, while praying for the day when she would break down and let him in. For some strange reason, she still held on to Carl, even after he left and never came back.

Old Man Johnson became Reggie's favorite person, even though he loved all of the Henley children the same. There was something about Old Man Johnson that made Reggie want to be around him all the time. Old Man Johnson saw the same thing in Reggie that Carl Jr. did-- someone who was misunderstood but special in his own way.

For a while, they lived the good life, with everything coming together. Even Old Man Johnson changed. Instead of sitting on the porch all night, he would turn in like a normal person. He hit the sack every night between nine and eleven o'clock, but only after he had called to check on the Henley household. He would get furious if no one was around to get his call. However, that never happened, because everyone knew how he was and didn't want him to come looking for them. Old Man Johnson acted like a grandfather to them, and he even took them to Reggie's home games, which became a family tradition.

It was the life Carl Jr. had always dreamed of, until Reggie's last year in school when everything made a drastic turn.

Carl Jr. remembered it like it was yesterday. He was working in the science lab with his one-of-a-kind chemical, when he received a phone call from Reggie.

"Hey, bro. It's me. You wouldn't believe who's sitting beside me right now. Jerry Parker, one of the NFL's biggest owners."

Carl Jr. paused for a moment because he couldn't believe what he was hearing.

"Bro, you hear me?"

"Yeah, I heard you. I'm just in shock right now."

"You were right, and I owe it all to you. You made me believe in myself and understand what a lot of faith can do to change a person's whole life. I love you, bro."

"I love you, too."

Reggie was the happiest man in the whole world at that point. He told Carl Jr. that one of the scouts said he was a first round draft pick, and had a ticket to just about any team he wanted. Excited, he asked Carl Jr. to call Barbara and tell her the good news because he had to talk with the owner. So, after hanging up with Reggie, Carl Jr. hurried and called his mother.

First thing she did was scream. "My God is a good God! Thank you, Jesus! My boy is going pro. He heard my prayers. Thank you, Jesus."

Carl Jr. felt good delivering the news. He had never heard his mother that excited about anything. It made his so happy that he wanted to cry. As he sat at his desk, he stared straight ahead and started reminiscing. For once in his life, the good times outweighed the bad. It felt so good that he got up and danced, shouted, and everything else.

He danced so hard that he knocked over two chemical test tubes and made a big mess. He didn't have any clue that the two chemicals would start a smoking reaction. Not knowing what was going to happen or what he should do, he started to panic. All he could think was, *I'm gonna catch this building on fire, and they're going to kick me out of school.*

He ran for the first thing that came to mind, the fire extinguisher, snatched it off the wall, and began to spray. He sprayed the contents of the fire extinguisher until finally the smoke cleared. He then sat down at the table, held my head, and took a few deep breaths. *What would I have done if I burnt this building down? Silly me*, he thought.

After bashing himself for being so careless, he began to clean the mess up. Grabbing the dustpan and broom, he started to sweep up the broken glass into one small pile. As he scooped it up, that's when he noticed nothing was wet. Carl Jr. bent down closer to see what had happened to the chemicals he had spilled, including all the gasses from the fire extinguisher.

God had found the answer to Carl Jr. prayers. What he had been working on for so long had come to him on a whim out of nowhere. It was unbelievable. The chemicals in the fire extinguisher were the answer to all his prayers. Like always, Carl Jr. was speechless.

Should I celebrate? Call my family and tell them the good news? Or should I keep it to myself until I really know this is it?

He thought long and hard for a couple of minutes before deciding not to celebrate until he had sold his first piece of jewelry. Besides, it was Reggie's time to shine. The last game of the season was two weeks away, and all the scouts were going to be there.

It was a madhouse in the hood. News anchors, sports magazines, local fans, and family members the Henley's never knew they had were there. It was crazy to see Reggie become famous overnight, and he sucked up all the attention from his fans. It was like no one ever knew his name until they heard the news.

Girls were everywhere. Even Ms. America called him. Carl Jr. couldn't believe all the attention one person could receive when they had money or were about to be blessed with money. Every one flocked to your every need. Everywhere you go, everybody knows your name. It sort of bothered Carl Jr., but he was happy for Reggie, who it didn't seem to bother one bit.

Even Michael started getting hit on by all the little girls at school once they found out Reggie was his brother. Not to mention, Old Man Johnson was so excited that he went out and bought the whole family jerseys with Reggie's number on it. Shakira and Faith didn't really know what was going on, so didn't much change for them. As for Barbara, she smiled from ear to ear every day when she went and came back from work.

One day, Barbara pulled Carl Jr. to the side and told him, "I could get use to this. Don't you know today at work, my boss called me to the office over the intercom? No one gets called to the office over the intercom unless they are either getting in trouble or getting fired. So, I was like, what now? When I got to his office, he told me to come in and have a seat. So, I went in and sat down with my heart beating faster than a runaway slave. Then he said to me, 'Do you know why you're here, Mrs. Henley?'

"I replied, 'No, sir, Mr. Peterson.' And that's when he went on to tell me that him and my floor manager have been watching me for a while now and felt I deserved a raise.

"Carl Jr., my heart skipped a beat. I couldn't believe what I was hearing. In the past eighteen years, I only had one raise, and it was for a whopping twenty-five cents. I was appalled. Not only did Mr. Peterson give me a raise, though, but he gave me a big one." Barbara paused and then said to Carl Jr., "Take a wild guess what he gave me."

Her son pondered for a second before blurting out, "He gave you a whole fifty cents?"

"Oh no," Barbara said. "He gave me a whole four dollars. Then he told me to keep up the good work and to take the rest of the day off. I had to pinch myself to make sure I wasn't dreaming. 'Oh no, it's real,' he had said. He told me to make sure I kept this to myself and then had his floor manager give me a ride home. You should have seen the looks the workers had on their faces as the floor manager escorted me to the door. They just knew I was fired."

Carl Jr. grabbed his mother and hugged her. "I'm happy for you. You deserve that and so much more."

"Thanks, my son," she said before shouting, "Thank you, Jesus! Thank you, Jesus! I knew one day He would answer my prayers." Then she started singing one of her favorite songs. "He may not come when you want him, but he'll be there right on time. 'Cause he's an on-time God. Yes, he is."

Carl Jr. knew deep down inside what was happening, but he didn't want to spoil the moment for her. The boss at her job was kissing up to his mother because he knew Reggie was about to go pro. If the boss was good to Barbara, he figured she could have Reggie come by the job, which would make him look good. It was just one of the many things that people gave in order to be included in their circle of friends.

It was like no one was real, and that bothered Carl Jr. a lot. He decided right then that if he ever got rich, he wasn't going to allow any of the people who didn't give him the time of day when he had nothing to smile in his face when he got something.

The charity went on until game day. Everyone and their mother were there. It was like the whole town had driven down to USC to watch Reggie play his last college game. Carl Jr., Michael, Shakira, Faith, Barbara, Old Man Johnson, and Joe were all sitting on the third row screaming and yelling, "Go, Reggie!" They were even wearing the new jerseys that Old Man Johnson had bought them.

It was a night to remember. Reggie played like he had never played before, breaking tackles and completing passes. He rushed for over one hundred and ninety-eight yards, and had three touchdowns in the first half. Scouts were going crazy, and Reggie's stats were going sky high. Even the fans were going nuts. All you could hear was, "Way to go, Reggie! Way to go!"

A scout ran down to where they sat and introduced himself to the family. "Make sure Reggie comes my way, and I guarantee you'll never have to work again," he told Barbara, who never said anything in response since she knew she had to be careful of vultures in the industry.

Halftime went by, and the teams made their way back onto the field, with the crowd screaming Reggie's name. On the first play of the second half Reggie threw a 78-yard touchdown. Talk about chaos.

Carl Jr. jumped up and down, yelling his head off. "That's my brother! That's my brother!" he shouted while beating Michael all in his chest.

The score was twenty-one to twenty-eight, in favor of Reggie's team with ten minutes left in the third quarter.

Clemson's very own Terry Dixon scored a 33-yard touchdown and got a two-point conversion, which made it a one-point game. Everyone got tense.

On the kick return, Reggie watched from the bench, trying to rest up for the fourth quarter. There were thirty seconds left in the third, and they hadn't scored. Now they had to punt to the other team. Coach called an onside kick hoping to recover the ball, but didn't. Clemson had the ball and the lead going into the fourth quarter.

Clemson got the ball spotted on the 30-yard line and plowed their way down the field. It seemed like every play was a run play. They were killing the clock. Six minutes into the fourth, Terry Dixon ran it in for a 10-yard touchdown. Clemson got the extra point and made it a nine-point game.

The pressure was on, and USC was counting on number fourteen, Reggie Miller. The ball was spotted at the 31-yard line. USC made their way down the field. You could feel the tension in the air as the Clemson fans went berserk. The play was in motion. Reggie faked and threw a bomb into the end zone, which was missed by Brian Fairwell, Conway High's All-American.

It was second and ten. The center over-hiked the ball, and number seventeen, Henry Allen, the fullback, recovered it. It was third and ten, and everyone screamed, "Give it to Reggie! Give it to Reggie!"

The play went in motion. Henry Allen ran up the middle on a fake. Reggie went to the left, faked a pass, and then took off like a bolt of lightning breaking tackle after tackle. He rushed for a 49-yard touchdown, and the crowd jumped out of their seats.

With less than two minutes to go, the coach called a timeout. This was the make-or-break play of the game. The fans were nervous as the team made their way back on the field. It felt like everything was in slow motion.

The play went in motion. It was the same fake, but Reggie was coming straight down the middle. They were going for the two-point conversion to tie the game. That's when everything went downhill.

Reggie dove over the top to meet Daryl Mitchell and Kevin Long in a collision. Kevin's helmet caught Reggie in the knees, flipping him over to hit Daryl's helmet in a head-on collision.

The crowd went crazy. The two points were good and the game was tied, but Reggie was not moving. Everything went sour. The coach ran out on the field. A minute went by, and Reggie still wasn't moving. They all started getting worried. It was like déjà vu.

"Not again," said Barbara. "Not again."

That's when the paramedics came out with a stretcher to carry Reggie off the field. He still was not moving. Everything went silent. As Carl Jr. glanced around the stadium, he saw players in the end zone with their helmets off and kneeling on one knee, holding hands in prayer as they took Reggie off the field.

This time, Barbara didn't move. Looking at Carl Jr., she told him, "Go check it out and make sure everything is okay. I can't do this again."

Without a word, Carl Jr. got up and made his way to the back, where he saw the assistant coach standing by the door with his arms folded and his head down.

"Is he okay?"

"Yes," replied the coach. "He's conscious, but his career looks like it ends here."

"What do you mean?"

"He busted both of his knees and has a major concussion. The doctor says at this point, he thinks it's over for him. His knees will never be well enough for him to play again."

Carl Jr. was devastated. How would he break the bad news to everyone? How was Reggie going to handle the fact that all he had worked so hard and so long for was over in one night?

The doctor made his way out the room and confirmed the bad news. With a hundred things running through his head, Carl Jr. knew exactly what Reggie was going to say, so he had to have his defense story ready. The whole time the assistant coach was inside the room with Reggie, Carl Jr. prepared himself for the worse.

Coach came out and told him, "You can go in. He's now up and aware."

"How is he taking it?"

"I can't really tell because he didn't say one word to me the whole time I was in there. Maybe you can get him to talk."

"I'll try," Carl Jr. replied, then made his way into the room.

There he was looking straight up in the air without a single expression on his face, as if he didn't see Carl Jr. come in. He walked over to his bedside and grabbed his hand.

"Are you okay, Reggie?"

He didn't even blink. Carl Jr. waited for a second and asked him again what was good.

"It's me, Carl Jr., your brother."

Like before, still no answer. He stood there confused, not knowing what else to say, as he held his hand in disbelief. He quietly turned his head, loosened his grip on Reggie's hand, and turned like he was about to walk out. That's when Reggie squeezed Carl Jr.'s hand real tight like he was holding on for dear life.

"Don't leave me, bro. I'm scared." With that, a tear rolled down his face.

"Don't be. I'm here for you all the way."

He turned his head in Carl Jr.'s direction. "Why us? Why us, Carl Jr.? What is it that the Lord has against us to always find a way to crush our happiness? How much more do we have to sacrifice before he truly answers our prayers?"

"I know it's hard right now, but you got to have faith."

Why did he say that? Reggie sat straight up and went into a rage.

"Faith! You telling me about faith? After all I've been through, you gonna come in here and tell me about faith? How much faith do I need? He has taken everything I love from me. My loving mother, my sister, my brand-new Phantom that I never knew was mine, and now my career. Don't tell me about no damn faith. I've been listening to you and your mother ever since we moved in. Faith ain't got us no damn where."

"Not true, Reggie. My God is a good God."

"You said it right, *your* God. He ain't no God of mine. As far as I'm concerned, there ain't no such thing as God. It's just a bunch of bullshit."

It was scary to here Reggie talk like that. The more he talked, the more he sounded like Carl, and the angrier Carl Jr. became. Reggie continued ranting about how God was this and that, until Carl Jr. couldn't take it anymore.

"You listen to me, dammit! I'm tired of you ranting about God and why he does what he does. You have no idea what He went through before he died for our sins. And you think the little hell you went through was something? Well, think again. You can't begin to imagine what He went through. Words alone can't describe the pain He went through for our sins. So, don't tell me about what you've been through, because in my book, you ain't been through shit. It's people like you that make it bad for the rest of us. Always crying about what's not right in your life and how God does you so wrong. Well guess what, homey? Get in line, 'cause there are a million other people out there screaming the same shit.

"Your father did it for years, and me and my family had to put up with that shit. He wanted to blame God for his mistakes, and he took it out on us. You saw him in action, and it wasn't just that day. There was something with him every day. I prayed every night for the Lord to take him out of our lives for good, and He did just that. Carl's been gone for years now, and no one misses him. So, don't tell me there ain't no God and he don't hear any prayers."

"Whatever, Carl Jr. You can go on believing that fairytale bullshit if you want. You're gonna be in the same predicament you're in now if you don't get off your ass and make something happen. Stop waiting on some make-believe man to come out the sky and change your life overnight. This shit out here is real. I've seen it all myself tonight. I went from being the town's greatest to the town's latest all in ten minutes. You think I don't know those people don't give a damn about me? Now that I'm not going pro, they're gonna give me their ass to kiss. Believe it or not, I prepared for this. I saw it coming. I knew it was too good to be true. That's why I never banked on faith. I believed in myself. That's what got me as far as I did."

Carl Jr. couldn't take another minute of Reggie's foolish talk. "You do what you got to do, Reggie."

"You damn right I am, homeboy."

After hearing that, Carl Jr. knew Reggie had something crazy on his mind. So, he ended the conversation and made his way towards the door, but there was one last thing he had to get off his chest before leaving the room.

"Reggie, I love you, brother, and I always will. No matter what you say or how you feel about me, I'm always gonna be here for you, and that's 'til death do us part."

Then Carl Jr. made his way out the door and slammed it behind him. He knew things were going to change, but he just didn't know how. He was no faced with the duty of having to break the news to his family. He waited until they were all loaded in the van and on their way home before telling everyone the bad news. No one made a comment but Old Man Johnson, and it wasn't a long one.

"My God, my God, spare us just for one chance."

After that night, Michael wasn't the man in school anymore. Old Man Johnson started sitting out on the front porch again. Barbara lost her job weeks after when her boss said he couldn't afford to pay her anymore and had to let her go. She only had five years left before retirement. Barbara cried for two days straight because her job was all she knew. She didn't know what to do.

Joe helped her through, assuring her that everything would be all right. He told her that if she wanted, her and the children could move in with him and stay there as long as need.

As for Carl Jr., everything was the same. He became consumed with making his jewelry because he knew that was the only way out.

Things were so-so for a while. No one had heard from or seen Reggie after the night of the game. Old Man Johnson worried himself to death about Reggie's whereabouts. He asked Barbara every day if she'd heard from Reggie because he knew how it felt to have everything he loved stripped from him.

Carl Jr. continued working day in and day out on his jewelry, trying to perfect every piece. Meanwhile Joe and Barbara were getting closer and closer. Carl Jr. even overheard Michael say something about divorce papers for Carl. He was glad to hear that his mother was finally letting go of his mean father. Every day was the same routine, until the day Barbara called Carl Jr. Immediately, he knew something was wrong.

"Hello, Carl Jr., it's me."

From the tone of her voice, he was scared to ask what had happened.

"Reggie came by today wanting to see Faith, and I told him he could. I asked him where he's been and what he's been doing. He said something about getting it in 'cause he promised Taisa he would take care of Faith. He then asked how you were doing and if you were still working on the jewelry 'cause one day he wants to be able to buy some. He looks like he's doing real good," said Barbara.

"Reggie pulled up in this big fancy car, and he left a big bag of money, which he said was for Faith's college. He'll be back to give me some more money just to put up for her. I told him she was good, but he insisted. He said he'd rather be dead than lie to his sister. I couldn't really say much about that. I know at this point nothing can change his mind."

Barbara continued. "I told Reggie that Old Man Johnson is worried about him, but he didn't even go by to see him."

"Mother, let him go, 'cause right now the only thing he got on his mind is fulfilling his promise to Taisa, which is something he will do by any means necessary."

"How can I tell Old Man Johnson that Reggie came by and didn't care to see him?"

"Don't, Mother. Just tell him that Reggie is not the Reggie he used to be."

Carl Jr. knew what Reggie was doing, but cared not to tell his mother because she wouldn't have taken the money. Carl Jr. planned to go home in a couple of days because he needed a break from all the jewelry stuff. He put in at least thirteen hours a day and some days even more.

*****

Knock! Knock!

"Who is it?" Barbara screamed.

Carl Jr. knew she was sitting in the kitchen by the phone because she knew it was time for him to call. He opened his cell phone and called at the same time he was knocking.

"Hello."

"Hey, Mother."

"Hold on," she said. "Someone's at the door."

She came to the door and opened it to see her oldest son standing there.

"Boy, I'm gonna kill you," she said while hugging him around his neck.

He didn't even get in the house good before she was pulling him to the back room.

"What is it?" Carl Jr. asked.

"I didn't want to say it over the phone, but I have been scared ever since Reggie left," she said. "He really left Faith a lot of money. I didn't think it was this much."

"How much is it?"

"I haven't touched it. I was waiting until you came home."

Barbara pulled the big bag from under the bed and poured it out. They were both speechless at the sight of so many hundreds and fifties. Carl Jr. counted two hundred and twenty thousand dollars, but he never told his mother exactly how much was there because he knew she would have had a heart attack. Barbara never asked where the money came from because she didn't want to know.

After waiting for nightfall, Carl Jr. took the money to his favorite spot in the woods and buried it like he did with all his other valuable possessions. He then made his way back to the house, only to see Old Man Johnson staring up into space as if he was looking to have a conversation with God.

"Hello, Mr. Johnson. Long time no see."

"You got that right."

"So what's been happening in your life?"

"As you can see, not a whole lot. Y'all kids have been driving me crazy. Y'all don't call, don't write, and don't even stop by to see how the old man is doing."

"I know, and I apologize. It's just I've been so busy working on my jewelry. I don't even have time for myself."

"Well, I guess that's the same story for everybody."

Carl Jr. knew what he was hinting around to, so he answered his question before he could even get it out.

"Mother did say Reggie came by last week."

"I know, and he didn't even stop by to speak."

"Reggie is going through something right now, Mr. Johnson. I don't think he wants to speak to anyone right now."

"You know, I kind of took a liking to that boy for some strange reason. It was like he was really my son. All y'all are like my children. It's just I knew he was alone, just like I was, and needed someone to lean on."

"He does, believe me. That's why he's acting like that right now. The person he wants to lean on isn't here anymore. Taisa was his everything, even when his mother was alive."

"Yeah, I know. He told me."

"Don't worry, Mr. Johnson, he'll be back around. Right now, he's on a mission. I just hope it works out for him like he plans."

"Me, too," said Old Man Johnson.

"Well, I have to go now. Mother is probably wondering what's taking me so long."

"Okay, Carl Jr. I'll see you later. That is, if you don't forget to come by."

"Oh, I won't. You got my word on that."

As Carl Jr. walked off, he could tell Old Man Johnson was hurting inside. It seemed like he wanted to share more, but didn't because he didn't want Carl Jr. to think he loved Reggie a little more than he loved the rest of the children.

CHAPTER 16

"Mother, sorry I took so long. I stopped by to see Mr. Johnson, and he isn't looking too good."

"Yeah. He's been looking that way ever since Reggie came by and didn't stop to speak to him."

"Did he say anything to you about it?"

"No, but I could tell he was upset."

"Me, too," Carl Jr. said. "I really wish Reggie would think of someone other than himself sometimes, and stop acting like the world owes him something."

"You know, he reminds me so much of your father it scares me, coldhearted and everything. That's why I try not to say much when he comes by."

"You don't have to worry about that. One thing I can say about Reggie, he's gonna make sure his family's okay. And that's by any means necessary."

"That's what scares me about him. Other than that, he's one of the most loving people someone could ever meet. I love Reggie, and pray every day and night that God will watch over him and bring him home safely. I'm not able to handle losing another one."

Seeing where things were going, Carl Jr. quickly changed the subject.

"So, Mother, how are things going with you and Joe?"

"What do you mean by that?" she asked.

"Well, a little birdie told me that someone got a divorce and Ole'

Joe has been coming by on the regular."

"I wonder who told you that."

"Oh, just a little birdie."

"Yeah, I know that little old birdie was no one but Michael," Barbara said.

"So, it's true?"

"Is what true?"

"You know."

"Know what?" Barbara said, acting clueless.

"That you and Joe are planning to get married, Mother?"

"I didn't say all that, but we have been seeing each other a lot lately. Every day seems so special."

"Okay, so what's the hold up?"

"It's no hold up. Just don't want to rush into anything right now."

"Mother, Joe has been chasing you for only God knows how long."

"Yeah, I know. It's just that after Carl, I look at all men different."

"That's because we are all different. Don't blame every man for one man's mistake."

"I'm not. It's just I need more time."

"Mother, time waits on no one. You've seen people all around you come and go. And a lot of them were unexpected. Don't ever second-guess your happiness. God knows you need a good man in your life. That's why he sent Joe. Someone who knows how to treat a woman. Someone who cares about your feelings. Someone who loves your kids as much as you do. Must I go on?"

"I know. I know you're right. He's a sweet guy. He's everything I can ask for in a man. It's just sometimes I think he's just too good to be true."

"Stop. Just listen to me for one minute. Didn't you tell me and all my brothers and sisters that God is a good God, and through him anything is possible?

"I did," Barbara replied while nodding her head.

"So where's the faith you've been preaching about for so long?"

Barbara didn't say another word as she made her way to her bedroom. Carl Jr. knew he had struck a nerve and that his mother was going to take a minute to talk with Jesus. While she was in her meeting with Jesus, he decided to surprise the kids and pick them up from school.

Carl Jr. headed down Old Chapel Road, only to run into bad traffic due to an accident. So, he decided to turn around and go the back way, not realizing what he was about to run into. As soon as he crossed 9th Avenue, he spotted Reggie standing in front of Joe's Poker Shack with two other guys. Carl Jr. slowly pulled into the backside of the parking lot, turned the car's ignition off, and began watching Reggie from afar.

He couldn't believe what he was seeing. He had a feeling Reggie was doing something, but he had the block on fire servicing crackheads, weed smokers, coke users, and God knows who else. Carl Jr. sat there for about an hour and watched Reggie make transaction after transaction. Not once did anyone recognize him sitting there.

Carl Jr. was so caught up that he forgot about picking the kids up. It's a good thing they weren't expecting him. Having finally seen enough, Carl Jr. decided to get out the car and approach Reggie. However, before he could get within a ten-foot range of him, the two guys cut him off.

"Are you lost?" one of them asked.

"No," Carl Jr. said, "just want to speak to Reggie."

"Does he know you?" the guy on the left inquired.

"Yes, I'm his brother."

"Brother? He doesn't have any brothers. The best thing for you to do is get the fuck up out of here before shit gets stank."

"No, I'm for real. That's my brother."

"Brother my ass, dude. You got to go."

Determined to speak to Reggie, Carl Jr. tried to go around the guy on the right, but when he did that, he soon found a gun pointed right in his face. Carl Jr. was convinced that if he didn't leave something bad was going to happen, so he made his way back to the car. He was puzzled because he knew Reggie had seen him, yet he didn't say a thing. The whole way home, Carl Jr. tried to figure out what had happened. After pulling up to the apartment, he headed to stairs.

"Hello, Carl Jr.," said Old Man Johnson.

"Hello," he replied.

"What's wrong? You look like you just saw a ghost."

"I'm good, just having a bad day," Carl Jr. responded.

"Well, let's talk about it. Maybe I can help."

"I'm good."

"Sit down and tell me what's bothering you."

"Okay, since you insist," Carl Jr. said, then started to explain what had happened.

"Oh, yeah," Old Man Johnson said. "He knows that's a no-no around here."

"But that wasn't what got me. Dude stuck a gun right in my face and demanded I leave, but Reggie never said one word. He acted like he didn't even know me."

"Are you crazy, Carl Jr.? Why would you get out your car and go up there? You know what kind of spot that is. Even the cops don't go up there. Someone gets shot or killed almost every month there, and no one hears or sees anything. If they do hear or see something, someone is bound to be found dead weeks later."

"Why didn't Reggie say anything, Mr. Johnson?"

"It's because when you're in a gang like that, no one needs to know you have family members. If they do and something goes wrong, the gang's not going after the person at fault. They're going after that person's family."

"I'm not scared of those punks, Mr. Johnson..."

Before Carl Jr. could finish his sentence, Old Man Johnson snatched him by the arm, pulling Carl Jr. close to him, and said, "You listen to me, son. Don't you ever in the rest of your years step foot up there. Those fools will kill you faster than you can blink and then come after your family. That's how they are. Don't think for one second they gonna let some young college boy stop that from happening. You know nothing about that life, so don't try to."

"I didn't realize it was that serious."

"Carl Jr., those people down there are trying to survive by any means necessary. That means they're ready to kill or be killed. Promise me you won't go back there. Promise me."

He looked up at Old Man Johnson and saw that cold look on his face. Slowly, he told him, "I promise."

"Go now," said Old Man Johnson, "and never speak of this incident to no one."

Carl Jr. turned around and made his way upstairs. As soon as he opened the door, Michael, Shakira, Faith, and Joe were all sitting at the table with big grins on their faces.

"Guess what, Carl Jr.," said Shakira.

"What is it?" he replied.

"Be quiet," Michael told her. "You always running your big mouth."

"Well, what is it? She already started to tell it."

"We're not going to tell it," Michael said. "We'll let Mother tell you."

"After the long talk we had, I prayed about things. Me and Joe are going to get married," Barbara informed her oldest son.

"For real?"

"Yes. Thanks to you, my son."

Joe grabbed Carl Jr.'s hand. "You don't know how much I owe you for this."

"You don't owe me a thing. All I ask of you is to make my mother happy because she deserves it."

"Oh, I will, and that's 'til death do us part."

Carl Jr. grabbed his mother and screamed, "Well, this calls for a celebration. I'm taking everyone out to eat, and it's on me."

"That's what I'm talking about," said Michael. "Red Lobster, here we come."

As they made their way downstairs, Carl Jr. told his mother that he was happy for her.

"Don't forget to stop by and tell Mr. Johnson the good news. See if he wants to come and celebrate with us," she instructed.

Carl Jr. knocked on his door and shared the good news, then asked if he wanted to come.

"No thanks, but tell Barbara and Joe that I'm happy for them. I won't miss that wedding for nothing in the world."

Carl Jr. could see it in Old Man Johnson's eyes that he was still upset about what he had told him earlier.

"Okay, Mr. Johnson, I sure will." After closing the door, he made his way to the car.

"Everyone ready?"

"Oh yeah. We're waiting on you," Michael said.

The whole way to the restaurant all Carl Jr. could think about was the gun in his face and Reggie doing nothing. After everyone was seated, he told them to order anything they wanted and not to worry about the cost. Of course, Michael was the first one to order.

"Well, I'm having lobster and shrimp with a side order of cheese sticks."

"Michael, don't be greedy," Barbara told him.

"Don't worry, I said it's okay. This is just the beginning."

Everything went lovely. Everyone was laughing and having a ball.

"These are the times I've been waiting on all my life. We're one big happy family, with everyone enjoying themselves," Carl Jr. said.

"Oh yeah," Barbara replied. "We appreciate everything you've done for us over the past few years. You really brought this family together."

"Not only that, you brought me and your mother together, and I thank you," said Joe.

"Well, he ain't done nothing for me," Michael voiced, "but bought me this delicious dinner."

"Whatever," Carl Jr. replied.

"Naw, I love you, bro," Michael said, getting serious. "I wish everybody had a big bother like you."

"Thanks. I couldn't have done it without you guys and of course God," Carl Jr. expressed, then excused himself to use the restroom.

"Don't wet yourself," said Michael.

"Calm down. You're in a restaurant," Barbara told him.

"Yes, ma'am."

After Carl Jr. made his way into the restroom, he noticed a black guy in the first stall, so he grabbed the next one and commenced to handle his business. Once he had relieved himself, he walked over to the sink to wash his hands. Since one sink was broken, he had to wait behind the guy who had been in the first stall. As soon as he finished, Carl Jr. washed his hands. When he reached to grab a paper towel, he noticed the guy from the first stall was staring directly at him. He paid him no mind and proceeded to dry his hands.

"Don't I know you?" the man asked.

Carl Jr. replied, "I don't think so."

"Are you some police or something?"

"No, I'm not the police."

"Then why the fuck are you following me around?" The guy seemed to be getting angry.

"Dude, I don't even know you," Carl Jr. told him, getting irritated.

"Don't fucking play with me. You know I'm that guy who stuck the gun in your face at the trap spot."

Once again, Carl Jr. was speechless. It was like staring death right in the face. All he could say was, "It wasn't me."

The guy looked at him for a second before saying, "If I find out that was you at the spot today, you better go get a black suit, because you will be going to someone's funeral. And that's on everything I love."

Holding his composure, Carl Jr. grabbed the door handle and replied, "Whatever."

By the time he got back to the table, his whole expression had changed.

"What's with you?" asked Michael.

"Oh, nothing. Just my stomach doesn't feel too good right now. It must have been the shrimp."

"No, you're just not used to eating this good. Come on, everybody. Let's get this big baby home before he throws up on everything. He's sick for real."

Carl Jr. paid the tab, and they headed home.

"Thanks for everything," said Joe. "I really had the best time of my life."

"Anything for my family," Carl Jr. replied.

He couldn't wait to go home to tell Old Man Johnson what had went on. As soon as they pulled up, Carl Jr. saw him sitting in his favorite spot.

"How was everything?"

"Oh, lovely," said Barbara. "You should have come."

"Maybe next time, but thanks for asking."

Carl Jr. fell behind, and once everyone was in the house, he began to tell Old Man Johnson what had happened. The whole time Carl Jr. spoke, he never said a word.

"What am I going to do, Mr. Johnson?"

"Nothing at all. Just keep this to yourself. Go home and try to relax. Hopefully tomorrow this will all be over."

Carl Jr. did just as Old Man Johnson said. He went upstairs and went straight into the bedroom to lie down, thinking, *what have I done?*

The next morning when he got up, Barbara had made a big breakfast.

"Good morning, my son."

"Good morning, Mother."

"Are you feeling better today?"

"Yes, ma'am. Not too bad."

"Well, put some of this real food in your stomach and maybe...just maybe...you might feel a whole lot better. Now, where's the remote? You know I got to watch my early morning news."

Carl Jr. turned the TV on to the news channel, and as soon as the picture came through, he saw the words *Breaking News* flash across the screen.

"Turn it up," Barbara told him. "I want to hear this."

The news anchorman reported, "This morning around 2:30 a.m., two men were found behind Joe's Poker Shack brutally beaten and stabbed to death. So far, police have no leads or suspects. Authorities are trying desperately to shut down Joe's Poker Shack for good. Here are pictures of the victims. On the left, Daryl Peters a.k.a. Long Shot, and on the right, Philip Gruesome a.k.a. Eight-ball."

Carl Jr. couldn't believe it. Those were the guys who had stuck the gun in his face and the one who had also approached him at the restaurant. He was so excited that he ran downstairs to tell Old Man Johnson about the guys being dead, but when he got down there, he wasn't there. At first, he didn't think anything of it, but by the end of the day, it began to dawn on him. *Could Mr. Johnson have killed those guys?* he wondered. *No, maybe it was just a coincidence, although I know he was capable of doing it.*

Carl Jr. never did get a chance to see Old Man Johnson because he had to head back to school. He had some jewelry to work on. All that week, day in and day out, he worked his fingers to the bone perfecting his planned craft.

It seemed like everything was falling into place. Barbara was getting married, and the family was safe once again. Still, Old Man Johnson worried himself to death about Reggie and what he had going on. Carl Jr. didn't worry as much because he knew eventually Reggie would come back round. And come back around he did.

His mother called him late one night and told him, "Reggie came back with another bag of money, bigger than before. He said it should last Faith until she goes to college."

"Did he ask about any of us?"

"Funny you ask that. He didn't mention anyone, and he left out quicker than he came in. I'm worried about him. He acts like he has a lot on his mind and never looks me in my face."

"Maybe he's just tired of running and ready to come home."

"I wish he would," Barbara replied. "I couldn't stand losing another one. This whole survival thing has got me whipped."

"I know, Mother, but like you said, as long as we got faith, there's always a light at the end of the tunnel."

"I know, my son. God knows what he's doing. When it's all said and done, we're going to be just fine."

They talked for another hour about the wedding, her excitement, and about Barbara and Joe not having the money they needed to have the wedding they wanted. Carl Jr. knew then that he had to do something. He had to get his jewelry on the market, and he had no time to waste.

When he got off the phone with his mother, he decided he would save the day by giving her the big wedding she dreamed of having.

CHAPTER 17

Carl Jr. remembered that night so well. He took a small picture of his jewelry and posted it on eBay with a price that was out of this world. He didn't expect anyone to bid. He just wanted them to recognize the new, one-of-a-kind jewelry. It was an once-in-a-lifetime offer since he only had one hundred pieces. He set the starting bid at four hundred thousand dollars per piece just to create a buzz while he worked on the rest of his collection.

Five days went by, and he didn't even bother to check it because he knew no one would bid on it. However, he received a phone call from eBay asking what he was selling that got a bidder to offer a million and a half dollars under the condition that he could see the jewelry in person. Once again, Carl Jr. was speechless, but he held his composure.

Carl Jr. was to meet him in downtown Manhattan on Saturday the 18th at three o'clock in the afternoon. The date was confirmed, and the only problem he had was trying to figure out how he was going to get there. He and the potential buyer had just spoken on Thursday, so he knew last-minute flights were very high. He also had to figure out clothes since he had to look rich selling something as expensive as his jewelry.

Immediately, Carl Jr. began panicking, until it dawned on him that the two hundred grand he had hid for Faith was the answer to all his problems. After grabbing his wallet, he used his last forty dollars for gas and made his way back home. The whole time while driving, he kept asking himself, "Am I dreaming? Could this really be happening?

Is God finally answering my prayers?"

After finally arriving at his favorite hiding spot in the woods, he dug up the money and headed back without stopping by to say hi to the family. He was on a mission. He had to get back before the bank closed. He had to deposit some big money and knew he couldn't deposit more than nine thousand dollars at a time. It was like God was on his side, because he got there five minutes before the bank closed.

"Hi, Mr. Henley. How can I help you today?" the bank teller asked.

"I want to deposit nine thousand dollars into my checking account."

She paused for a minute. "Are you sure you don't want to put it in a savings account?"

"Yes, I'm sure."

"What about a CD? We have excellent interest rates right now."

"No, I'm good, but maybe next time."

Without any further questions, she processed the deposit.

Next, Carl Jr. headed to the mall, where he purchased a two-thousand-dollar Armani suit and a pair of five-hundred-dollar Armani shoes. He also bought a nine-thousand-dollar Rolex, a three-thousand-dollar pinky ring, and a bottle of Versace Blue Cologne. He was in business. Once home, he went online and booked a first-class ticket. Then he reserved a five-star suite at the Grande Regal Royal in the heart of Manhattan, with a 24-hour limo to take him everywhere.

While sitting there for a few minutes, he came up with a whole new list. He needed an expensive briefcase to carry his expensive jewelry and a bodyguard to watch his back while he made the deal. *Who can I call?* he thought. Before he could answer himself, the campus security guard drove up by the dorm window making his routine stop. Carl Jr. took off down the stairs after him like someone was trying to kill him.

"Excuse me, sir, can I have a word with you?"

"Sure, and you are?"

"Oh, my name is Carl Henley, Jr. I'm a student here."

"Nice to meet you, Carl. I'm Jason Parker, a retired state trooper trying to keep myself busy."

"Well, Mr. Parker, this is going to sound a bit strange, but I was wondering if I could rent you for the weekend to be my bodyguard for a business trip."

"And where might you be going?"

"New York."

"New York?"

"Don't worry, I'll pay for everything. A first-class plane ticket, a five-star hotel in the middle of Manhattan, and five hundred dollars a day."

"Wait a minute. You mean to tell me that you're going to pay me five hundred dollars a day to be your bodyguard and pay all expenses?"

"Yes, sir. I'll book the ticket right now in front of you and give you two hundred and fifty dollars up front."

"I don't know about this. It sounds too good to be true."

"That's what I said, but it's happening. Are you in or what?"

"I would, but it's just that I have to work this weekend."

"I'll tell you what, you call in and I'll double your pay. I'll give you a thousand dollars up front. Not only that, if the deal goes through, I'll give you a full-time job for two years paying a hundred thousand dollars a year. I'll put that in writing."

"You really are telling the truth, aren't you?"

"Yes, sir."

"Okay then. You have yourself a deal, as long as it's not illegal."

"No, sir. This is all me. I've been working on this since I started school here."

"Okay, take my number and call me tomorrow. If you show me the plane ticket and a thousand dollars, you have yourself a deal."

"Say no more, Mr. Parker. Tomorrow it is."

Carl Jr. took down all his information, went back upstairs, and booked his tickets.

That whole night he didn't get any sleep. He couldn't believe this was really happening. After tossing and turning for most of the night, it was soon 6:25 a.m. on Friday morning. First thing he did upon getting out of the bed was to call Mr. Parker.

"Hello?"

"Hi, Mr. Parker. It's me, Carl. I have the tickets and the money. Where do you want to meet?"

"You can meet me on 3rd Avenue at the old coffee shop. Say around 7:15 a.m."

"Say no more. Seven-fifteen it is."

At seven o'clock on the dot, Carl Jr. was there waiting patiently, and at seven-fifteen on the dot, Mr. Parker pulled up dressed in all black and looking like a secret service agent.

"Is this the look you were looking for?"

"Yes, sir. That's exactly what I'm looking for." Carl Jr. handed him the tickets and money. "The plan is to leave at six o'clock tonight."

"See you at six then," he said, then added, "I hope what you got going works out for you."

"Oh, it will, Mr. Parker. I've got faith, and I know this is it."

Carl Jr. returned to his room and gathered his things because he wouldn't have time to go back since he still had some running around to do. I went to the Gucci store and purchased a thousand-dollar briefcase to carry his jewelry in. Then he deposited another nine thousand dollars in the bank. He packed twenty thousand dollars in his Gucci briefcase before heading for the airport.

He arrived there at five o'clock, and Mr. Parker pulled up at the same time. As they walked to the counter together, Mr. Parker grabbed Carl Jr.'s bags.

"Let me, sir," he said. "You just hold on to your briefcase."

They then made their way to the metal detector, where their tickets and I.D. were checked.

"Briefcase, please," said the security guard who stood in front of the x-ray machine. "We have to run it through the scanner."

With the briefcase halfway through the scanner, the security guard stopped the moving belt. "Step to the side."

Mr. Parker looked concerned about what was going on, but he

maintained his composure.

"Mr. Henley, we have to open your bag because something is giving off a funny signal. Do you mind?"

"Of course not."

They opened the briefcase, pulled back the suede cloth, and revealed the sparkling piece of jewelry.

"Wow! What is that?" the security guard asked.

"Oh, it's some jewelry I'm about to sell to a client I have in New York."

"This is unbelievable," he said. "Look at the crystal shine on this jewelry and the way it's shaped. Do you mind if I let the others see it?"

"No, go ahead. Be my guest."

Before the guard could take it, though, Mr. Parker grabbed the top of the briefcase and closed it. "That won't be necessary. We have a plane to catch, but thanks for the compliment." He then placed the briefcase back in Carl Jr.'s hands. "After you," Mr. Parker said.

Carl Jr. couldn't believe it. Mr. Parker was treating him like he was somebody of high importance.

When they arrived at their departure gate, they sat there patiently waiting to board. The whole time while sitting there, Mr. Parker never asked to see what Carl Jr. had in his briefcase.

"Now boarding Flight #13, heading to New York City at gate four," the airline stewardess announced over the intercom. "Arrival time is scheduled for 9:45 p.m. at Jefferson International. May we ask only first-class ticket holders to board at this time."

Carl Jr. and Mr. Parker got up and made their way to the plane, while people stared like they were looking at a star and his bodyguard. It was a feeling beyond feelings for Carl Jr. After everyone boarded, the flight crew sectioned off first-class seating and gave them special treatment. Carl Jr. loved every minute of it.

Soon, they landed in The Big Apple. After getting off the plane, they made their way to the baggage claim area. When they got there, there was a man holding up a sign with Carl Jr.'s name on it. Mr.

Parker grabbed the luggage, walked over to the man, and said something to him.

"Right this way," Mr. Parker turned and said.

Outside, there was an all-white stretch limo with another guy standing there holding the door open. Carl Jr. looked at Mr. Parker because it wasn't the limo he had ordered. The one he had ordered was all black.

As if reading his mind, the guy came over and said, "I know this isn't the one you ordered. This limo was sent by Mr. Alicastro, the one who's buying the jewelry from you."

"It's okay," Mr. Parker said. "I spoke with the other guy. Mr. Alicastro knows him, too."

When they got into the limo, there was a fancy bottle of champagne and two beautiful women to serve it.

"Drinks anyone?"

"No, thanks," said Mr. Parker. "My boss doesn't drink nor smoke, but he would like to go to a fine restaurant."

"Anything you want," one woman said, "compliments of Mr. Alicastro. You name it; we got it. If not, we can find it. What would you like to eat?"

"Well, I want a nice steak dinner."

"Steak it is," she said as the limo pulled off from the airport.

Ten minutes later, they pulled up to a fancy restaurant in the heart of Manhattan. They stepped out like some made men. As soon as they got inside, Carl Jr. saw a table with his name on it. *How could it be? They didn't know we were coming,* he thought.

Mr. Parker leaned over and whispered in his ear, "The limo driver made a call on the way."

"Is this how it is when you have money? Everything catered to you."

"Only when you have real money," replied Mr. Parker.

"I could get use to this."

Carl Jr. ordered a steak and a side of potatoes. Honestly, it was the best steak he ever had in his life. After dinner, the driver asked if they wanted to do something else. Carl Jr. looked at Mr. Parker, who answered for him like he could read his mind.

"No, thanks," he said. "We'll just head to the room and prepare for our long day tomorrow."

"Hotel it is," said the limo driver.

When they arrived at the hotel, Carl Jr. pulled out a hundred dollars to tip the limo driver, but he refused to take it.

"Mr. Alicastro took care of all that. Here is my number to call no matter what time of day or night it is."

Mr. Parker took the number and followed Carl Jr. to the room. "I'll sleep on the couch," he said.

"But I bought you a room."

"I know, but I have to make sure nothing strange happens to you until the deal is made."

"Say no more. I'll see you in the morning."

As soon as Carl Jr. hit the bed, he went straight to sleep and slept like a baby. Probably because he felt safe knowing Mr. Parker was not far away on the couch.

The next morning, Carl Jr. woke up around 11:45 a.m., having already missed breakfast.

"Why did you let me sleep so long?" he asked.

"I knew you needed the rest. Besides, I want you to be on point today. I ordered you something to eat," responded Mr. Parker, "and it's already on the way. In the meantime, let's go over the game plan."

"What game plan?"

"The one you're going to need in this meeting. To do business, you have to know business, and knowing business is the key to success."

Mr. Parker and Carl Jr. went over the game plan for two hours, with the hired bodyguard teaching him how to keep a straight face, how not to seem desperate, and not to be afraid to say no. They practiced all the way up until it was time to get dressed. That's when Carl Jr. pulled out his fancy gear.

"Wow," said Mr. Parker. "You weren't playing around. Now that's how a boss man is supposed to look."

"Oh, you thought I was playing?"

"No, not really. Just didn't know you were coming like that."

After getting dressed, they made their way downstairs.

"Did you call the limo driver?"

"Yes, sir, I did."

"Great. Don't want to be late for this important meeting."

"Oh, we won't, boss," Mr. Parker replied.

CHAPTER 18

They pulled up to a huge, all-glass building, walked in, and were escorted to the top floor. Once they stepped off the elevator, they saw that Mr. Alicastro's office took up the whole floor. When they walked in, a woman greeted them.

"Please have a seat. Mr. Alicastro is expecting you." She then leaned over and spoke into the intercom. "Mr. Henley is here, sir."

"Send him in."

Nervous, Carl Jr. was shaking in his boots, but remembered everything he and Mr. Parker had gone over.

"Hello there, Mystery Man," said Mr. Alicastro. "So you have something I want?"

"Of course I do, or I wouldn't be here, right?

"Absolutely. Let's cut through the bull crap. Where's the million-dollar jewelry you were talking about?"

Carl Jr. placed the briefcase on the table and popped it open. When he pulled back the suede cloth, Mr. Alicastro's eyes lit up like a neon sign.

"Mind if I take a look at it?"

"No, help yourself. Try it on if you like."

He called his assistant and had her put it on him. "How does it look?" he asked her.

"It's unbelievable. This is like something I've never seen before. It's just unbelievable."

"This is truly a one-of-a-kind piece, and it's a must have," Carl Jr. told him.

"Say no more," responded Mr. Alicastro, then told his assistant, "Cut the check." Looking back at Carl Jr., he said, "Nice doing business with you."

"You can deposit the money into my bank account," Carl Jr. told the assistant. "I'll call back when it gets in there."

"No, I'll call you," she said. "Mr. Alicastro says he would hate to find out that more than a hundred pieces were sold or find out someone has one just like his."

"You have my word on it. Money back guaranteed."

"It's not the money he's worried about, Mr. Henley. It's the rarity."

"Like I said, he has my word on it."

"Okay. Nice doing business with you. Have a nice day."

"Oh, we will," said Mr. Parker.

Carl Jr. couldn't wait to get back to the hotel. He felt like a balloon full of hot air waiting to burst.

As they got into the limo, Mr. Parker said, "I'm not going to ask what just happened because I was there and saw what happened, but I still didn't believe it."

"Me either," Carl Jr. responded, "but it's not over yet. We haven't received the money."

"I don't think he's the kind of guy who would bullshit someone."

"Neither do I, but I can't celebrate until I know the money is there."

Carl Jr. started feeling sick from being so nervous. He didn't know if it was really going to happen.

When they got back to the hotel, Mr. Parker asked him if he wanted to go out for a tour of the city.

"No, the curiosity is really killing me."

"Don't worry yourself about that. You told me before we got here that you knew if he saw it, it was going to be a done deal."

"I know, Mr. Parker, but we're talking about a million dollars here."

"It doesn't matter if it's ten million. If it's supposed to be, then that's what it's going to be. Besides, what happened to the faith you were talking about?"

"You're right. Let's go out and celebrate. Everything's on me tonight."

Mr. Parker called the limo and told the chauffeur to show them the town.

"Whatever you want," said the limo driver.

It was on. They rode around the town and stepped out like they were millionaires. It was unbelievable. The things Carl Jr. saw were unreal. These people were on a whole other level. They witnessed things some people would never see or even dream about seeing.

Time flew by, and before they knew it, it was one o'clock in the morning. Carl Jr. was starting to wind down, and Mr. Parker could see it in his face.

"You ready to head back to the hotel?"

"Yes, sir," Carl Jr. responded. "The night is over for me. Tomorrow is the big day when I become a millionaire and you become my full-time bodyguard."

"Sounds like a plan to me," said Mr. Parker. "So to the hotel it is."

Carl Jr. looked at the front entrance of the hotel, not knowing how he got there. That's just how tired he was. He couldn't wait to jump in the bed, money or no money. He was out like a light within five minutes. Morning came quickly.

"Rise and shine, Mr. Henley. Today is the day."

He peeped his head from under the pillows. "What time is it, Mr. Parker?"

"One o'clock in the afternoon."

"No way. I couldn't have slept that long."

"Oh yeah. You were sleeping like a baby, so I didn't bother you."

Anxious, Carl Jr. got dressed as quickly as he could. He had to go see if the money cleared. Knowing the money he was spending wasn't his, the deal had to go through. Just then, his cell phone rang, and without thinking, he quickly answered.

"Hello. Carl Jr. speaking."

"Is this Mr. Henley?"

"Yes, it is."

"Well, I'm a representative for Coastline State Bank, and I was told to give you a call. A deposit in the amount of one-million-five-hundred-thousand dollars has cleared."

Carl Jr. dropped the phone and couldn't say a word.

"What is it?" Mr. Parker asked as he picked up the phone to listen to the rest of the conversation. By that time, the representative was saying have a nice day.

"Who was that, Mr. Henley?"

Still in a state of shock, Carl Jr. remained silent. Finally, the words slowly eased out of his mouth.

"The money has cleared."

"Are you serious? The money really cleared?"

Carl Jr. never said a word. He just stared off into space, while thinking to himself, *Thank you, Jesus! Thank you, Jesus! You heard my prayers.*

"My hard work and faith finally paid off. Now my family will never have to struggle again," he spoke out loud in a happy voice. "No more rundown projects. No more living in fear. No more working like a slave. The pain is over."

Mr. Parker cut in. "I don't believe this. This is too good to be true. I bumped into you, a kid with a wild idea who didn't know what to expect, took a chance on it, and stepped out on faith, and now I'm going to be making a hundred grand a year as your bodyguard. God is good."

They looked at each other, paused for a second, and then started jumping up and down, while screaming, "We're rich! We're rich!" They did this until they wore themselves out.

"What now?" Mr. Parker asked.

"We're catching the first thing smoking back to South Carolina."

"But our plane doesn't leave until six o'clock tomorrow."

"Who cares? We'll buy a last-minute ticket. I'm rich now."

"Say no more. You're the boss."

Mr. Parker grabbed their things, called the limo, and soon, they were headed to the airport to catch the first flight leaving, which was scheduled to depart in the next hour.

"Two first-class tickets to Myrtle Beach, South Carolina," Carl Jr. told the ticket agent.

When she told him the price, he whipped out the money, threw it on the counter, and told her to keep the change. She handed them the tickets, and they were on their way home. They had arrived just a few minutes before the flight took off and made their way down the tunnel in a flash, boarding in the nick of time. Carl Jr. took his seat by the window and stared out of it, thinking of all the things he was going to do for his family when he got back.

The first thing on his list was to give his mother the biggest wedding she could ever imagine. He also planned to build her a big house she always dreamt about. He would set aside Michael and Shakira's college funds. Also, he wanted to build Old Man Johnson a two-bedroom guesthouse right next door to his mother's home. Most certainly, he would make it his business to find Reggie, tell him that he had made it happen, and convince him leave the streets alone and to come home.

Once they arrived at the airport in South Carolina and walked outside, there was a limo waiting and a man holding a sign up with his name of it. Carl Jr. was confused because he never ordered a limo and neither did Mr. Parker.

"Wait here," said Mr. Parker as he made his way over to the limo driver to see what was going on.

They conversed for about a minute. Then he looked back and yelled, "It's all good."

When Carl Jr. got over to the limo, Mr. Parker explained, "The limo is from Mr. Alicastro. He said it was nice doing business with you and that he'll be contacting you to do more business in the near future."

After jumping into the limo, Carl Jr. told the driver to head to Joe's Poker Shack.

"Joe's Poker Shack?" asked Mr. Parker.

"You heard me right. I'm hoping to see my brother so I can bring him home. Are you with me or not?"

"I took the job, didn't I? Say no more."

As they pulled up at Joe's Poker Shack, Reggie was standing in the same spot doing his usual thing. Everyone looked at the limo, wondering who was inside. Carl Jr. made sure the driver pulled the limo up so close that no one would cut him off this time. Mr. Parker got out and opened the door. As Carl Jr. stepped out with his fancy suit and gold Rolex looking like a million bucks, Reggie's eyes got big as quarters.

"What's been happening, bro?" Carl Jr. asked while walking towards him.

Reggie hesitated to say anything, knowing what happened the last time.

"Relax," he told him. "You don't have to hide no more because we're leaving the hood for good. I'm rich now."

Reggie just stood there before asking, "Who's the guy in all black?"

"Oh, that's just my bodyguard, Mr. Parker."

Reggie couldn't believe it, but when he looked Carl Jr. dead in his eyes, he knew he was telling the truth.

"Come home, Reggie. It's over now. You don't have to do this anymore. Now you can come home and help raise Faith like you promised you would."

Reggie never said a word as tears rolled down his face. "I miss my family, Carl Jr. I'm tired, but out here is where I belong. These people need me."

"No, Reggie, we need you. It ain't a day that goes by that we don't worry about you. Even Mr. Johnson misses you. He said you were like his own son, and he became closer to you than any of us. Now it's

134

killing him to know you're out here on these streets trying to make a difference. We love you, bro, and we always will. No matter where you go or what you do, we're going to always be here for you."

"Go home, Carl Jr. This is it for me. This is all I know."

"No, dammit, don't tell me that. I've known you for more than most of my life, and I know this is not all you know."

"I knew football, Carl Jr., and look where it got me. Nowhere. I caused our mother to lose her job after all these years, knowing damn well that was the only thing she knew."

"That wasn't your fault. Don't blame yourself for that. Ain't nothing promised out here no more. One day you can have it, and the next day it's all gone. That's why when we do get it, we're going to enjoy every minute. You never know when the day will come and it's all gone."

Carl Jr. grabbed Reggie by the wrist, squeezed it tight, and looked him dead in his eyes.

"Reggie, I'll tell you like my father told me, the only thing in this world that is promised to us is death. So, if you think standing out here doing what you're doing is going to last forever, then you're dead wrong. I need you. The family needs you. And I'm not leaving here without you."

"I'm not going anywhere, Carl Jr. I told you this is it for me."

Carl Jr. turned around and hit the limo window with his open palm.

"Cut the limo off," he told the driver. "Mr. Parker, we're going to sit here all day until Reggie gets his ass in this limo and promises me that he'll never come back to these streets again. If he doesn't, I'm going to come here every day, all day until he makes that change."

Reggie grabbed Carl Jr. by the shirt and shoved him against the limo with tears rolling down his face and his eyes bloodshot red. "Don't make me go there."

He looked up at Reggie with a cold look in his eyes. "Do what you have to do. I'll be damned if I lose another family member to some bullshit."

Reggie stood there for a minute trembling like he was ready to explode. He then grabbed Carl Jr.'s neck and hugged him as tight as he could, while crying his heart out.

"I promise, Carl Jr., when I leave this block, I will never turn back."

Carl Jr. cried as hard as he did. Mr. Parker opened the door, got the two into the limo, and told the limo driver to head to the projects. They cried the whole way there, never looking back.

"I love you, bro."

"I love you, too, said Reggie. "I thank you with all my heart for standing up to me and making me realize it's not all about me. It's about those who love me."

CHAPTER 19

Reggie paused for a second, staring out the limo window, and then quietly spoke. "I see you made it happen, bro."

"I sure did. We're gonna live it up from here on out. All I ask for you to do is just sit back and enjoy the ride."

When they pulled up to the front of the projects in the long, white limo looking clean, everyone ran up to see who was inside. It was like they were movie stars.

"Reggie, come up last so we can surprise the family," Carl Jr. told him.

Mr. Parker stepped out, opened the door for Carl Jr., and guarded him like he was the president. He walked him all the way to the apartment. Everyone was shocked to see it was Carl Jr. who got out the limo. People were whispering to each other trying to figure out what was going on.

When they reached the apartment door, Mr. Parker knocked.

"Who is it?" asked Michael, yelling from inside the kitchen.

"Mr. Parker, Carl Jr.'s bodyguard."

The door flew open, and there stood Old Man Johnson with a mean look on his face. "Mr. Who?"

Before he could ask him again, Carl Jr. stepped from behind Mr. Parker. "It's me, Carl Jr."

Barbara stepped up. "Who is this man with you, and why is he dressed like that?"

"Long story," Carl Jr. replied.

"Oh, don't worry, I have all day."

It was perfect. Carl Jr. didn't have to look for anyone because everyone was already there.

"What's the big occasion?" Carl Jr. asked.

"Oh nothing. I just decided to cook a big dinner for the family."

"Why wasn't I invited?"

"Because I knew you were in school, and you only come home twice a month." Barbara replied before quickly jumping back to the Mr. Parker situation. "Carl, who's this man, and why is he just standing there like that?"

"In a minute, Mother. Gather around, everyone. I have a big surprise."

"It better be a good one," said Michael. "You're interrupting my dinner."

Carl Jr. looked at Mr. Parker and nodded his head, giving him the go ahead to get ready.

"What on God's earth do you have going on?" Barbara asked. "You come home in the middle of the week dressed in this fancy suit, and the man with you doesn't smile or say anything. He just stands there stiff as a board in the middle of our living room."

"In a minute, Mother. Let me surprise the family first."

Everyone patiently waited for Mr. Parker to return with the big surprise. Two minutes later, footsteps could be heard coming up the stairs.

Knock! Knock!

"Come in," said Barbara.

The door opened slowly, and everyone stood in suspense. Mr. Parker stepped in first. Reggie, who was three steps behind him, held his head down like he was ashamed to face the family. Reggie walked in and everything went sour. Reggie lifted his head up to look at everyone with tears in his eyes.

"Sorry it took so long to come back to my senses, but thanks to Carl

Jr. being the brother that he is, I realized it's not all about me. I have a family who loves me unconditionally, and no matter what, y'all always have my back. Sorry I let y'all down. Sorry I wasn't here for y'all. I never stopped loving y'all for one second. I thought about each and every one of y'all every minute of the day. But, I felt like I was doing the right thing by staying away because I didn't want what I was doing to cause trouble on my family."

"We understand," Old Man Johnson told him. "We know you meant well. We were just worried about your safety. Praying everyday that no one would call and say that you were killed or locked up for doing something crazy."

Afraid that things might start to go downhill, Carl Jr. quickly changed the subject. "Enough about that. He's here now, and that's all that matters. He promised me that he'll never leave us again, and if he does, I have permission to bust his head open."

"Carl Jr., what in the world did you just say?" Reggie said, knowing that his best friend/brother was only half-joking with his statement.

"Can we eat now?" asked Michael.

"No, I haven't finished with the surprise yet."

"Well, what is it? I'm starving."

Everyone gathered around and prepared for the big news.

"Okay, remember when I told y'all that I was working on this fancy chemical for one-of-a-kind jewelry? Well, it happened. I sold my first piece for a million-and-a-half dollars."

"Is that what you had me waiting on for all this time?" Michael said. "A not-so-funny joke? Let's eat, everyone."

"It's true," said Mr. Parker, finally speaking. "I wouldn't have believed it myself if I wasn't there. And, by the way, I'm his bodyguard."

"Bodyguard!" yelled Barbara. "What kind of trouble are you in to have a bodyguard?"

"I'll explain that later," Carl Jr. said.

"You mean to tell me you have a million dollars!"

"Yep, and it's all in my bank account. So, from here on out, things are going to change. First thing is to leave these projects and never look back. That goes for you, too, Mr. Johnson. Tonight is the last night we're staying in these rundown projects. Pack what you cherish the most and leave the rest behind."

"What about my clothes and my bike?" Shakira asked.

"Leave it. We're buying all new things. I don't want anything to remind me of these old projects. You've got one hour to take what you can. The limo will be outside waiting."

Michael ran to the window. "Oh my God! He's really telling the truth. We're rich for real! I'm ready now. I don't want anything. I'm getting all new things."

"Whatever you like. Y'all got one hour, and I'll be back."

"Let's go," said Mr. Parker. "We've got some hotel hunting to do."

Carl Jr., Reggie, and Mr. Parker rode around looking, laughing, and talking about their future.

"Reggie, if it wasn't for your money, I wouldn't have gotten here. I'm going to give you every dime of it back."

"Don't worry about the money. Keep it," he replied while looking at Carl Jr. "I know you'll do the right thing with it."

Forty-five minutes went by, and they finally found a place that would sleep about sixteen people. It was perfect, with eight bedrooms, five and a half bathrooms, Jacuzzi, pool, game room, and a spectacular view of the ocean. Mr. Parker handled all the paperwork since Carl Jr. didn't have a major credit card. When the paperwork was all done, they made their way back to the projects.

As soon as they pulled up, Michael and Shakira ran down the stairs with not one thing in their hands. Barbara and Joe came down with the baby and a few other things. Everyone was ready except there was no Old Man Johnson.

"Mother, what's going on? Why isn't he ready?"

She looked at him with a sad look on her face, and right away, Carl

Jr. knew he wasn't coming.

"Let me talk to him," said Reggie. "I think I can get him to change his mind. Y'all just wait for me in the limo."

Reggie knocked on his door, but got no answer. He knocked again, and still no answer. This time, he yelled, "It's me, Reggie, Mr. Johnson!"

Like magic, the door opened. Old Man Johnson stood there, eyes full of tears, holding on to a little brown box.

"What's wrong? Why aren't you coming?"

"I'm afraid," said Old Man Johnson. "I haven't left these projects as long as I can remember. I don't even know what the outside really looks like. I haven't dealt with people other than y'all for a long time. I don't know if I can cope."

"Don't worry about that. We're here for you like you were here for us, and I promise I'll never leave you again."

Old Man Johnson grabbed Reggie around his neck and hugged him like a baby. "I've never loved something as much as I love this family. I was afraid to think if something ever happened to y'all I wouldn't make it."

"The storm is over, and the sun is going to shine for a long time now. We're a family, and we're going to be together for the rest of our lives. No more running away. No more being apart. It's our time now, and we're gong to live it to the fullest."

Old Man Johnson grabbed his coat, threw his key on the floor, and said, "New beginning."

Everyone jumped up and down when they saw both of them heading towards the limo.

Things were on the up and up. Barbara and Joe planned their wedding, while Carl Jr., Reggie, and Old Man Johnson looked at house plans. They ended up purchasing ten acres from Mr. Parker for little to nothing. He was just happy to see them together as one big family. Carl Jr. had it mapped out: Barbara, Joe, and the kids in the middle house; Carl Jr. and Reggie in the two side houses; and Old Man Johnson in the guesthouse out back. It was perfect. They had their own mini-subdivision that they named the Henley Park Estates.

However, money was going fast. Carl Jr. didn't realize how fast money went when you don't have anything. Five hundred thousand was gone just that quick, and he hadn't even looked at furniture yet.

Carl Jr. was getting worried. He hadn't gotten any more bids on the pieces he put up the week before, and time was running out. He was checking every day on the hour, but still no bids. It wasn't until the last day during the last hour and thirty-two minutes that he started getting bids like clockwork. It was crazy. In thirty minutes, he had twenty-one different bids for amounts over a million dollars. *This can't be happening,* he thought.

He even received a call from a guy who told him that if he stopped the bid, he would buy both pieces for five million dollars.

"I was told to tell you Mr. Alicastro sent me," the caller informed him.

Immediately, Carl Jr. stopped the bidding because he knew the money was good. Once again, he and Mr. Parker headed out to make the transaction. This time, they weren't as anxious. It was all strictly business. They arrived, and an hour later the deal was done. The deal was good, the money was good, and they were living the life.

After returning home, Carl Jr. had an interior decorator lay out the house from top to bottom. He also purchased six Mercedes, two suburban XL's, and an RV. It was unbelievable. No one outside of the family had a clue on how or where Carl Jr. was getting his money. All they knew was the Henley's were on the come up. Everything they wanted was within the reach of their fingertips. It was unreal. Over six million dollars off of three pieces of jewelry, and Carl Jr. had a hundred more pieces to sell.

Next, he auctioned off a five-piece set, starting the bidding at five million dollars. Before he could get a bid, though, he received a phone call with a set price and was told once again that Mr. Alicastro had referred him. Money was coming in hand over fist. Every time it seemed like the price doubled. Carl Jr. was getting money faster than he could spend it.

Barbara and Joe put a rush on their wedding since money was no longer a concern. Reggie was so loaded that he didn't know what to do. He rode around all day flashing money and showing off his fancy cars and trucks with the big rims, hollering at every girl he saw.

Michael played video games like crazy and bought Jordan shoes every other weekend. Shakira had sleepovers every Friday, ordering pizza and everything else under the sun. Joe stopped driving cabs and became a house dad. Barbara started skipping church because every Sunday her and Joe would go shopping for things they didn't need.

What was going wrong? It was like no one had time for anyone. It became so bad that no one even noticed Old Man Johnson had stopped sitting outside to read his paper. It was getting ridiculous.

Carl Jr. called a family meeting, but to his surprise no one showed up. Everyone had prior engagements. That is everyone except Old Man Johnson. Carl Jr. saw him sitting on the front porch when he drove up. He walked over to speak, and that's when Old Man Johnson told him that he noticed things changing, and that everyone was too busy.

"I haven't seen anyone in about a month. I think they've almost forgotten that I'm back here. Ever since you put that money in our bank accounts, everyone has been going nuts. I sit here day in and day out watching them change right before my eyes. I don't even know who they are anymore. Barbara did stop by a couple of times, asking if I was hungry and if I wanted to come over to eat, but every time I get ready to go over, Joe comes up with a reason to go out and spend more money.

"I noticed the children's grades dropping. Faith's always at the daycare, and Reggie thinks he's some kind of pimp. That's why I hesitated on leaving where I was. It's like I'm lonelier here than I was there. At least I saw people coming and going. Lord knows I'm happy we've made it out, but making it out seems like it's just tearing us apart. Back then, I guess all we had was each other, which is something money can't buy."

"It's all my fault," Carl Jr. said. "I should have never given them that kind of money in the first place. Now that's all it's about…money, money, money. We're not even a family anymore. I'm tired of doing business deals. I never have time for our family, and everybody wants something. Before I got rich, some of these people wouldn't even speak to me. Now I'm their best friend. If I would've known this money would change us like this, I would've never prayed for it."

"It's not your fault, son. That's what money does to some people."

"Why didn't it do me like that?"

"Because your head was someplace else and you just wanted everyone to be happy. Trust me, they are. It's just that right now, they are enjoying things they've never had. It all gets old, just like anything else. Just pray. When it does get old and they understand that money isn't everything, they'll realize money can't buy happiness. Carl Jr., continue to prosper, and don't blame yourself for any of their actions.

"You did what you set out to do, and that was to provide for your family. I think you're a very fine young man who would do anything to see his family happy. I can see it in your eyes. The only thing I ask of you is to never sacrifice yourself for someone else's pleasures. God is the only one that can save the world. Know that no one is perfect. As long as you live, put God first and believe he's the ruler of all rulers."

Carl Jr. sat there, staring off into space, soaking up every word, trying to make sense out the whole money thing. He realized that Old Man Johnson was right. He had done his part; the rest was on them.

CHAPTER 20

Months later, things started going downhill. The money thing was out of hand, and the only person who seemed to not change was Mr. Parker. Carl Jr. guessed it was because he took it as his job. As for Carl Jr., it was all still a dream because he never had time to enjoy any of it. He was always on the road doing deals. He was making more money than he could count. The funny part is it seems like when you have money everything is free.

Everywhere you go, when people find out who you are, they cater to you hand and foot. To Carl Jr., trying to figure out who was real and who was not was becoming annoying. Everybody had a motive, and it seemed like the only reason they were around him was for personal gain. He trusted just about anybody. Mr. Parker always tried to tell him about his new so-called friends, but he was always a bit naive.

"How can someone be like that knowing I'm not? I keep it real with people, even the ones I barely know."

"Not everyone likes you. I respect that, and that's why I'm here doing this job. I do it as if I just started yesterday and haven't asked for a dime since the day I started."

Carl Jr. knew he was right, but he didn't want to hear that because he really liked hanging out with most of his *so-called* friends. However, it was becoming a nightmare for him. He had it all: money, cars, women, whatever he wanted. Still, he wasn't happy. He tried not to think about it too much because it was making him more and more depressed.

Needless to say, Carl Jr. kept making deal after deal because he knew his family had to eat. If he didn't come through, he knew that would make them sad. And if that happened, they would be back where they started.

Things at home didn't get better. Michael came home from school scared to death, saying some guys had robbed him for his sneakers. Shakira lost her best friend because she wanted to hang out with the rich kids. A live-in nanny was raising Faith, and Old Man Johnson took sick. But, Carl Jr. had no time to stop. He had less than half of his jewelry sold, and his phone was steady ringing off the hook.

Barbara and Joe decided not to have a big wedding. Instead, they wanted to get married on an island and fly around the world for their honeymoon. Once again, like always, Carl Jr. was speechless. The whole money thing was taking a toll on him. Everybody was happy except him, and he was the one making all the money. He felt like he had to help everyone with a story, including all his close friends that had it made. They knew anything Carl Jr. had they could get and that he never asked for anything in return because he thought that's what true friends do.

Carl Jr. wasn't dumb, though. He knew most of them were out for what they thought he could do for them, and the rest of them wanted him to believe they were one hundred. Still, he continued to do for them despite what anyone said. It got so deep that a couple of times a few of them told him that they would die for him. Now how real was that? Or was it real at all? It was confusing. It broke him down until one day he went off the deep end.

He remembered it like it was yesterday. He was sitting in his room drinking some Louis the XIII and watching *The Color Purple,* when all of a sudden, he became real depressed and felt like his mind had started slipping. He started asking himself questions that he couldn't answer. This went on for almost an hour until he reached his breaking point. He didn't know who he was or what he was there for. He was scared and needed someone to talk to. He wanted to go to his mother's house and tell her what was going on, but when he got ready to go, he forgot how to drive. He had the keys in his hand, but he forgot what they were used for. So, he went back inside, laid across the bed, and tried to pull himself back together, but it started getting worse.

I'm going crazy, he thought to himself. Then he jumped back up, made his way back to the car, opened the door, sat down in it, and grabbed the steering wheel, staring at it with the keys in his hand. Five minutes later, he realized the keys went in the ignition. After inserting the key into the ignition, it came back to him vaguely. He cranked the car up, threw it in drive, and attempted to drive to his mother's house. Good thing it wasn't far, because he drove approximately five miles per hour all the way there.

When he got there, he forgot how to turn the car off. He sat there for a minute before it came to him. He then turned the car off and made his way to the door. When he went to knock, Barbara had already opened the door.

"What's wrong? You've been standing there with your hand up for about two minutes, but you never knocked."

All of a sudden, he started crying. "I feel like my mind is slipping away from me."

"No, boy, don't you say that. Your mind isn't slipping, and you're not going crazy."

He couldn't stop crying. Barbara grabbed him and held him tight as her tears fell on top of his head.

"Lord, no!" she screamed. "Not him, not my boy."

He could feel his mother's heart beating faster and faster the harder she cried. It was killing him to know his mother was hurting because of him. That's when he fought hard to pull himself together.

I'm not crazy. I'm not crazy. I'm not crazy. The more he said it, the stronger he got.

Barbara kept crying, praying and begging the Lord to help her son. Carl Jr. knew he had to pull himself together.

"I'm okay now. I'm going back home to lay down."

Barbara grabbed his face and looked him dead in the eye. "Go home, get down on your knees, and pray. Pray until you can't pray no more. It's nothing in this world worth losing another child, and I would trade it all in to have my boy back."

He made his way back to the car while still trying hard to pull himself together because he knew his mother was watching from the doorway. He put the key in the ignition, started it, and made his way to the house, but by the time he got there, he started having different thoughts.

What if I go crazy? What will people say about me? Will they think I took some kind of drug? Would they know the real reason? Would it tear my mother apart?

The more he thought, the more drastic he became. He thought about ways to ease the pain and shame. Then it dawned on him---suicide. If he killed himself, no one would have to suffer. No one would have to take care of him. It was the perfect answer.

When he got home, he went to his dresser, pulled out his nine millimeter, and loaded a clip. He sat there for about ten minutes contemplating, until he finally built up enough courage to do it. Carl Jr. slowly put the gun up to his head, closed his eyes, and began to count to three.

One…two…three.

He pulled the trigger, but the gun didn't fire. When he lowered the gun to see what was wrong, someone was banging on the door and screaming. Carl Jr.'s car was rolling down the driveway and into the yard across the street.

In a daze, he opened the door and said, "I think the keys are in it. If you get it, you can have it." Then he turned around, shut the door in his face, and looked into the mirror. All he could see was his mother crying her heart out, telling him to give it to Jesus. So, he got down on his knees and did exactly what she told him to do. He prayed and prayed, until he had prayed himself to sleep. When he woke up the next day, he was scared to get up. He waited for about thirty minutes, asking himself questions to see if he knew the answers. Afterwards, he jumped in the shower and turned on the cold water to make sure he wasn't dreaming. After taking a shower, he got dressed and went to the door to take a look outside. His car was dented, and there was a note stuck on the windshield that read:

Dear Mr. Henley,

I don't know what happened yesterday, and I'm not going to ask. The keys were left in the ignition, and the car was in neutral. It rolled down the driveway and crashed into the statue in the neighbor's front yard. I got in your car and pulled it back into your driveway. I locked the door, and I have the key with me. I can be reached at 843-555-0000.

Your neighbor,
Madison

P.S. I hope you feel better.

He quickly called Madison to come over, and once he arrived, Carl Jr. asked him what he had said. He looked at Madison standing there holding the keys in his hand, not knowing what to think or what to say.

"If I told you that, why did you bring the car back?"

"Because it's not mine, and I knew something was going on with you. So, I did what I thought was right."

"Madison, how old are you? Do you have a license?"

"Yes, sir," he replied with a smile.

"You don't have to call me, sir. If you retrieved the car, then the car's yours. I'll have the title put in your name within two days. If your parents have any questions, tell them to give me a call. In the meantime, you should have someone fix that dent in the trunk."

The look on Madison's face was like that of a young child on Christmas morning. "Are you for real?"

"Yes. Now go ahead before I change my mind."

"Yes, sir, Mr. Henley," he said, then he ran to the car and rubbed his hand across the hood.

Carl Jr. went back inside, sat on the couch, threw his hands behind his head and knew he was back to normal thanks to the man upstairs. He had a new outlook on things.

I'm going to help those who help themselves. There are no more freebies.

A week went by, and things began to change drastically. Those who he thought were his friends disappeared when they found out the money had came to a halt and they couldn't use him for anything anymore. They dropped off faster than dead flies. Some stuck around because they used their money wisely and didn't need him anymore, while others just fell by the wayside.

Carl Jr. didn't sweat it much, though, because he had bigger problems dealing with his family. Just when he thought things couldn't get any worse, it hit rock bottom. It started with Reggie getting a call from the DEA. They said a witness claimed he saw Reggie murder two guys behind Joe's Poker Shack a while back, and he had to be brought in for questioning.

Old Man Johnson found out he had cancer, and the doctor said he didn't have long to live. Barbara canceled her trip around the world and came back to her senses after Carl Jr.'s freak accident. She started going back to church, but things weren't looking good at all.

Reggie didn't say much to anyone. He just started staying home reading the Bible, asking the Lord to get him out of the mess he found himself in. When he wasn't doing that, he was sitting on the porch with Old Man Johnson talking and watching Faith run around the yard. It seemed like it took all that for them to become a family again. No one cared about the money anymore. It was all about the family now.

Carl Jr. stopped selling his jewelry and had Mr. Parker take over the business. He knew he could trust him to do the right thing because he was the only one who hadn't stiffed him.

Things were going bad and good at the same time. Barbara was taking it hard, blaming herself for turning her back on Jesus when she got blessed. "The Bible says that money is the root of all evil. All I want is my family back how it used to be before all this money came," she had said one day.

Every day after that, the family grew closer as Old Man Johnson got worse. Reggie's court date was just around the corner, and it seemed like waiting on death itself. Carl Jr. could see it in Old Man Johnson's eyes. He was hanging on by a thread. It was like he was just trying to hang on until Reggie's court date. Carl Jr. never asked Reggie if he really did it, because every time someone mentioned it, he got nervous and locked himself in the house for hours. And Carl Jr. never conversed with Old Man Johnson about it because it was eating him to death.

Time was winding down. Reggie had court in three days, and Carl Jr. had to know the truth. It was eight o'clock Friday night, and Reggie was just getting in from Old Man Johnson's house. Carl Jr. pulled up as he was unlocking the door to the house.

"What's happening bro?"

"Oh, not a lot. About to go in here and relax a little," Reggie replied.

"Mind if I come in?"

"No, come on. I need some company to get this court stuff off my mind."

That was Carl Jr.'s cue to pop the question. "Speaking on that, I've been meaning to ask you…"

Reggie cut him off. "I know. Like everyone else, you want to know if I did it, right?" He hesitated and then asked him, "Do you want the truth, or do you want the story I told my lawyer?"

"I want the truth."

"Carl Jr., you can't handle the truth."

"Trust me, I'm a big boy now. I can handle more than you think."

Reggie looked him dead in the face. "Yes, I did kill those two guys.

You satisfied now?"

"What in God's name would make you do something like that?"

"Remember that day you saw the guy in the restaurant bathroom and he asked you were you the police?"

"Yes."

"Well, that was my partner, and he was planning to kill our mother. He followed you from the restaurant, found out where you lived, and put a hit out on our mother. But, he had to check with me first. I couldn't say anything because I didn't want him to know we were family. If he did, he would have killed us both. I asked him could I go because I felt like you were trying to set me up. I knew it wouldn't be long before they found out the truth, so I had to act fast. That night, I sat in the backseat with my gloves and mask on and a long pocketknife, acting like I was going to kill that lady and make you pay.

"I rehearsed the killing over and over, knowing I couldn't make any mistakes. To kill the both of them, I had to move fast. We sat there getting amped. I pulled out a bag of blow to get them right before we got there, and that's when I made my move. I gave it to the driver first to take his hit, and when he passed the bag, I grabbed his mouth and slit his throat. When the passenger had the straw to his nose, I stabbed him dead in the throat. I made sure both of them were dead, and I fled the scene. Lord knows I didn't want this to happen, but I couldn't take a chance of letting them hurt my family. I would rather be dead."

"Damn, Reggie, why didn't you go to the police?"

"If you think for a second the police give a fuck about you and some drug dealer, then you got another thing coming. By the time they would have responded to that, our whole family would've been dead. If you wouldn't have brought your ass down there in the first place screaming that you were my brother, this would've never happened."

"Oh, you're blaming me now?"

"I'm not blaming anybody. I'm blaming myself. I did it, and if I'm found guilty, I'll have to do the time. There's not one day that goes by that I don't regret what I've done. I watched those guys hurt a lot of people for a lot of different reasons, and it would have only been a matter of time before I was next."

Carl Jr. stood there trying to think of ways to help. Reggie could see the stress on his face.

"Don't worry, it's in God's hands. The only thing I can do now is wait."

Carl Jr. went back home, laid down, and prayed all night, asking the Lord to forgive Reggie and give him a second chance. Time was running out, and the family had no idea that Reggie was guilty. Carl Jr. was scared to death.

*****

There was one day left before the trial began. That night, Barbara called a family meeting, and this time, everyone was there except Old Man Johnson. Carl Jr. figured he was tired of them not showing up and decided to not show himself. Barbara also noticed he was not there.

"Carl Jr., go see what's wrong and make sure he is alright."

Barbara wanted everyone present for this meeting, so Carl Jr. quickly ran over to Old Man Johnson's house and knocked on the door.

"Come in, Carl Jr.," he said in a low, sad voice.

"How did you know it was me?"

"I was looking out the window and saw you run across the lawn."

"Mother wanted me to check on you and see why you aren't at the meeting."

"I'm not feeling too good, and I have to get my mind ready for tomorrow. This court thing is really stressing me out."

"Me, too. I haven't slept in days."

"I know, son, but don't worry. He's not going nowhere. I just hope this time he learns something from all this."

Carl Jr. didn't say anything because he knew Old Man Johnson didn't know Reggie was truly guilty. He could see it in Old Man Johnson's eyes that he was barely hanging on. It was like death was staring Carl Jr. right in the face. For some strange reason, he began to get nervous, and Old Man Johnson seemed to be getting weaker and weaker by the minute.

"Are you okay?" Carl Jr. asked him.

"I'm fine. Only a few more days, and I'll be heading home."

Carl Jr. knew exactly what he meant, because he had heard that same line from Taisa, but now was not the time. He quickly changed the subject.

"I'm heading back to the meeting. Hope you feel better."

Before he could get out the door, Old Man Johnson asked, "Do you still have the key I gave you many years ago?"

Carl Jr. turned around real slow. "Yes, of course, I do. Why would you ask?"

"I've been to the doctor again. He told me that I'll be leaving here real soon because there's nothing else they can do for me."

"Who cares what the doctor says? God is the real doctor. He's the only one that can make that call, not them."

"It's okay, Carl Jr. I'm ready to go. I've got my soul right with God. I've asked him to forgive me for all my sins."

"No, Mr. Johnson."

"Yes, Carl Jr. I know it's been a long road with you and the family losing a lot of loved ones. But, have you ever thought it was all done for a reason? It took me meeting you all and losing Reggie to get right with God. I tried for many years to figure this thing out, and it just wasn't happening until I found out Reggie could be facing some time and the family began falling apart. I had to call on Jesus and ask him to help me out of this mess. I can't go on no more. I surrender.

"That's when I heard a voice in my head. For a minute, I thought I was tripping. He told me that I'd worn my angel completely out and that they've been trying to reach me for a long time. God told me that he knew my heart, things I thought only I knew. He told me the times he had to step in and save me. I realize there really is a God, and he knows everything."

Carl Jr. watched the tears roll down his face as he continued.

"All these years, I've been searching for happiness. Mad with the world for taking my family, not realizing my family was in a better place. I know now God works in mysterious ways, and I am not to question him."

He reached out his trembling hand, and with tears still rolling down his face, he looked Carl Jr. dead in his eyes and said, "Carl Jr., life is worth living only if you have something to live for, and dying is just something that's bound to happen. The real joy is Heaven, a place where many strive to go... a place that Earth will never compare to... a place where tears are the tears of joy... a place where death takes a permanent holiday."

Carl Jr. stood there with tears rolling down his face, too, but this time, they were tears of joy. He felt good and at peace with himself.

"Go now, my son. Tell everyone that I'm okay and that I'll see them tomorrow at the trial. I have to rest up because it's going to be a long day."

Carl Jr. wiped the tears from his face as he headed towards the door.

"I love you, Carl Jr., and I always will."

"I love you, too, Mr. Johnson," he replied, then closed the door behind him.

He made his way back to his mother's house only to see the meeting was over.

"What took you so long?" asked Barbara. "We waited and waited, and you never showed up."

"I'm sorry for that. It's just that Mr. Johnson had a few things to get off his chest. But, other than that, he's doing just fine. Better than he has been in a long time. He told me to tell you that he's getting some rest for tomorrow and will meet us there."

"That's fine," Barbara replied. "All we can do now is wait on Jesus."

Everyone hugged and went their separate ways, trying to hold it together for the next day. On Carl Jr.'s way out the door, Reggie hugged him again.

"No matter what happens, I love you and the family with all my heart. If it takes my freedom for your lives, then so be it."

"Don't worry, Reggie, it's in God's hands now."

"I know. That's why I'm not worried either way it goes down. God's got my back, and there's nothing in this world that can change that."

Carl Jr. went home, laid down on the bed, and started reminiscing about all the times him and Reggie had shared, the good ones and the bad ones. Before long, he had cried himself to sleep.

CHAPTER 21

Not knowing what the outcome was going to be for Reggie made it real hard for everyone. Barbara cooked a big breakfast that morning, and everyone showed up except for Old Man Johnson. No one bothered to ask this time. They probably just figured he wasn't feeling too good.

It was strange at Barbara's house that morning. No one really said that much to anyone. Time was winding down, and court was in the next hour. Before making their way to the courthouse, they all gathered in a circle outside and said a prayer. As they loaded up in their cars, Barbara asked Carl Jr. to go see if Old Man Johnson was ready. When he got there, there was a note on the door that read:

To whom this may concern,

I have already left. See y'all when you get there.

Signed,
Mr. Old Man Johnson

After he told his mother what the note said, they were on their way to the courthouse. When they got there, a sheriff's deputy was taking Reggie back to see the judge. Not five minutes later Reggie was back out with the verdict.

"What happened to the trial?" asked Barbara.

"I really don't know," Reggie replied. "The witness changed his story at the last minute and told them that he was the one that did it because he was tired of seeing those drug dealers ruining his city."

This time, everyone was speechless.

"So, that's it?" Michael asked. "You can go? You're a free man now?"

"Hell yeah," said Reggie.

Carl Jr. couldn't believe what was happening because he knew Reggie had done it.

"Let's go celebrate," Michael suggested.

"Good idea," said Joe. "Let's get out of here before they change their minds."

It was like a real live party. Everyone was jumping up and down, while screaming, "Reggie's a free man!"

Still, Carl Jr. was confused. He felt deep down that something wasn't right.

"Party at my house," said Reggie, "and everything's on me."

It was unbelievable. Just that quick everything was back to normal. Everyone went right back to what they were doing before this happened. Barbara looked at her oldest son and nodded her head as if she knew he was thinking the same thing.

"Wait a minute here. What's wrong with all of you? Everyone is jumping up for joy and praising themselves, but no one has given a word of thanks to Jesus. Have you all not learned anything from all of this? "

"Oh yeah, thank you, Jesus," said Reggie, then Michael, then Shakira, and then Joe.

Seconds later, they went right back to partying. Carl Jr. had seen enough and was ready to go home and lay down. When he got home, there was a message on his answering machine, so he played it back. It was a call from the county jailhouse.

"Carl Jr., it's me, Mr. Old Man Johnson. By the time you get this message, I will have already been processed. Come down to the county jail alone, and I'll explain the whole thing to you."

Carl Jr. jumped in his car and drove as fast as he could to get there, only worrying about getting him out. All kinds of things ran through his head. *Did they finally run him down for killing that family? Did he kill someone else? What is going on?*

When Carl Jr. got there, he was already stressed out. He asked the lady at the front desk if he could speak to him.

"Come back tomorrow around four o'clock."

"I can't wait that long."

"Sir, you have no other choice. See you tomorrow."

Carl Jr. was sick. He didn't know what he was going to do? Returning home, he laid down for a minute, hoping to calm down, but it only got worse. He had to tell someone what was happening. So, he jumped up, called his mother, and told her to come over because he didn't want anyone else to know what was going on.

"I'll be there in a minute," she told him.

When she got there, Carl Jr. was pacing the floor.

"Okay, what's going on?" she asked.

"It's Mr. Johnson. He's in jail."

"What?!"

"Yes, he's in jail, and no one can see him until tomorrow at four."

"What did he do?"

"I don't know. I never got a chance to talk to him."

"Why didn't you ask someone? They would have told you."

"I don't know," Carl Jr. replied. "I guess I wasn't thinking clearly."

Wasting no more time, Barbara called the jail and asked if they had an Earl McJohnson and about his charges. Carl Jr. never knew Old Man Johnson's real name.

"Yes, ma'am," said the clerk lady. "He was sentenced to fifty years in prison for the double homicide of two drug dealers that happened a while ago."

Devastated, Barbara looked at Carl Jr. with tears rolling down her face and her hand over her mouth. It was crazy. How could he get charged with something Reggie did?

Barbara cried like a baby, not saying much of anything. Carl Jr. made her promise not to tell anyone until he had a chance to talk with Old Man Johnson. His mother sat there for a while until she got herself together and then went home. This time, Carl Jr. wasn't speechless. He was confused.

That was until he got a phone call at 2:45 a.m. He received a call from the county jail telling him that they were rushing Old Man Johnson to the emergency room. He had told them to call Carl Jr.

He quickly got dressed and rushed to the hospital. When he got there, he asked for Old Man Johnson and was told he was in ICU. It wasn't looking too good.

The doctor came out to the waiting area shaking his head and told Carl Jr., "Any day now he'll be going on."

Carl Jr. went to the room to where Old Man Johnson was hooked up to a heart monitor, an IV, and other various machines. He sat beside his bed and watched him sleep. Soon, Old Man Johnson woke up smiling and happy to see him.

"Hey, Carl Jr."

"Hey."

"I know you're trying to figure out what's going on."

"You already know."

He turned his head towards Carl Jr. and told the story. "I know and you know that Reggie killed those kids. I thought about it long and hard before I decided to do what I did. When I look at Reggie, I see a confused young man that's trying to hold on to something he really knows nothing about. He means well, and he really has a big heart. He would do anything, and I mean anything, to protect this family. Even if it means giving up his family."

"I know, but why you?"

"Carl Jr., I've lived my life. In my lifetime, I've done a lot of things that I'm not proud of, but I have asked for forgiveness and the Lord answered my prayer. I got a second chance. Now, I have the ability to give Reggie a second chance like He gave me. I'm dying, Carl Jr., and I know it won't be long. So, I figured if I turned myself in for those murders, it could never come back and haunt him again."

Never in a million years would Carl Jr. have figured that out.

He then said, "I want you to promise me that you won't tell anyone about this. This is our little secret."

"I promise."

He grabbed Carl Jr.'s hand and then started smiling and crying at the same time. Carl Jr. could see him fading away right before his eyes.

"I have something I've never told anyone else, and I have to get it off my chest."

Old Man Johnson looked at him with a warm, shallow look and said, "Speak."

Carl Jr. looked around the room to make sure no one was there and then began telling his secret.

"Remember how my dad used to beat us, take the bill money, call my mother all these names, and make her feel bad?"

"Yes, I do."

"And remember how you had to put him in check for stressing us? Remember when you said one of these days he was going to leave and we were going to have a better life? Well, it all began to come true that day. My dad tried to beat me again, but I took off into the woods to my favorite hiding spot. That same day, he told Mother that he was sorry for having us, and that he was going to leave and never come back. Not knowing he was behind me the whole time as I ran, he waited until I got to where I was going, and then he jumped out and tried to grab me. When he did, he tripped over a tree limb and hit his head on a big rock. It was crazy. For one time in my life, I felt like I had the upper hand. He was so tough, but you should have seen him begging for me to help him up.

"'Please, son. Please, son, go get help. Daddy can't move', he had begged me. That's when I said, 'Oh, so now you're my Daddy?'

"He shouted, 'No, son, please don't do this! Go tell your mother

I'm hurt'.

"That's when all hell broke loose. I thought about all the things he'd done to Mother. The physical and mental abuse he'd put her through and then he wanted her help. Not this time. I knew if he went back, our lives would be a living hell all over again, and that was not about to happen. I picked up that same rock he hit his head on, stood over him, and began to hit him in the head over and over and over until I knew he was dead. It was like the world was lifted off my shoulders.

"I sat there smiling, staring off in space and thinking to myself we were free. Thank God! I knew I had to get rid of the body, so I dug a hole about four feet deep, threw him in, and covered him up with dirt. Every day for a month, I went back and added more dirt until I had a big hill. No one ever suspected anything because I was always back there. I knew for a long time I was going to do something with his remains. I just didn't know what.

"By the time I was in 9th grade, I knew exactly what I was going to do. I studied the human bones for many years and knew if I could come up with some kind of chemical solution, I could beautify the bone and be a rich man."

Old Man Johnson grabbed his hand and squeezed as tight as he could. "Ask the Lord for forgiveness, for you know not what you've done."

Carl Jr. loosened his hand as Old Man Johnson's grip grew weaker and weaker. Then he stood up and told him, "Remember you told me that one day my dad would be worth something to me? You were right. The jewelry I sell is made from my dad's bones."

Before Carl Jr. could turn the knob to leave, Old Man Johnson passed away. As he looked at his body slowly changing color, he reminisced about all the good times they had together. About all the times Old Man Johnson had helped his mother and all the times he had looked out for him. Carl Jr. considered Old Man Johnson his "true" father, the man his dad was supposed to be. Old Man Johnson raised Carl Jr. to be the man he was today.

Carl Jr. looked out the window and saw it was starting to rain. As he gazed out the window, he saw a beam of light coming through the clouds. It was then that he knew everything was going to be okay. Carl Jr. knew Mr. Johnson was still looking over them, just from a different place. He straightened his tie, held his head up high, and walked out the hospital and into the sunset.